GATHERINGS FROM THE GOOD EARTH

A MONTH-TO-MONTH COLLECTION OF MUSINGS, FOLKLORE, RECIPES AND MORE

TWILA K. FAIRBANKS

Good Earth Publishing

CONTENTS

MARCH

APRIL

MAY

JUNE

JULY

AUGUST

SEPTEMBER

OCTOBER

NOVEMBER

DECEMBER

IN THE BEGINNING

Look deep into nature and you will understand everything.
-Albert Einstein

I AM a child of the earth. I take off my shoes and feel her heartbeat through the soles of my feet in the dark green grass. We are part of each other.

I contemplate many things — Earth's beauty, her future and destruction, and what my grandchildren and great-grandchildren will learn from her. She has much to teach us if we listen, meditate and are silent. Her secrets are everywhere and each person, in their own time, will unlock those secrets and find the truth and wisdom in what they need for healing in these uncertain times.

The earth is what we all have in common.
-Wendell Berry

IT WAS TIME to write everything down in one place. I wrote for many years in a journal, scrapbook, notebook, and calendar, remembering important things each month as I lived the year. I have been collecting the names of the moons and their meanings for the past twenty years, which I shared in my monthly newsletters for my *Log Cabin* shop friends. The positive feedback from those who read my newsletters was appreciated and led me to this point. I want to thank all of you, my Nebraska *Log Cabin* shop friends and the friends of my Estes Park shop, *The Sampler*, who took the time to tell me how much you appreciated the newsletters. Even after I moved away, I was encouraged by many to keep writing or write a book of my musings. I am touched that you enjoyed my writings and miss them since I no longer have a shop and have gone through many changes in my life. You are the best, and what good memories we all have of the *Log Cabin* and *The Sampler* shops. You are the ones who encouraged and supported me after my husband died and I needed to make changes in my life. You have known of my love of nature — the herbs and plants in my garden that give me food and medicine, the trees, the animals and birds that frequent the places I live. Thank you.

Wherever you are, it is your friends that make your world.
-William James

THE TIME HAD COME to pull all those newsletters, notes and journals together. For me, writing a book was like birthing a baby – and I have birthed a son and a daughter. This labor was much longer – almost ten years as I debated about writing a book or not. I did not share my dream with anyone for many of those years. It was buried deep within as I quietly gathered my essays and journals and continued to write each day. And when I laid awake at night writing in my sleepy mind, I made countless outlines, which added life to the dream.

During that time, my life changed in a dramatic way when I lost my husband unexpectedly. The brain fog and depression were intense, and I threw away some of my writings. I did not want to do anything, let alone write. And then one day, two years later, I gradually started writing in a daily journal as I had done before. I knew writing was good therapy.

I wrote to express my love of living close to the land, my deep gratitude to Mother Earth for her healing, and my learning to live mindfully each day of each month of each year. Living mindfully each day within each season made me always aware of what was happening around me in the plant and animal world where I lived. I would sit with a plant and talk to it and listen for its reply. I heard the singing in the tree branches above me, and I could hear ancestral voices guiding me.

I have lived on the prairie and plains of Nebraska and in the Rocky Mountains at 7800-foot elevation, and now I live in the woods and hills of Kansas (yes, there are woods and hills on the eastern edge in the land of Oz). My homes have been varied, and living in a log cabin was my favorite.

MY CHILDHOOD PREPARED ME FOR A LIFE OF HAVING A connection with the earth. I came from frugal, "salt-of-the-earth," self-sufficient people who farmed for a living day in and day out, morning to dark. Nature was our teacher growing up, and the land produced the food we ate.

My siblings and I climbed the mulberry trees, eating the juicy fat berries that stained our hands and clothing. We climbed the trees because we enjoyed climbing and we liked the view. We would peer into a bird nest to see the eggs and later the tiny birds waiting to be fed. The wheat field beyond was a joy to run through when the breezes ruffled the wheat grass like undulating waves of an ocean. When the corn grew six-feet tall we could play hide and seek, except sometimes we could not find our way out of the maze of stalks, and we yelled at the top of our lungs, *"Come find me, I'm lost!"* Playing in the hayloft and throwing loose hay at each other was kid's play and itchy. We looked for toads and frogs and watched caterpillars and were amazed at butterflies. Those many years ago we played outside from after breakfast in the morning until dark at night in the summer. There was much to do outside, and our imaginations ran wild — we could be king of the mountain (a dirt pile) or the queen of Sheba, or a zookeeper, or whatever we could think of. We knew the garden had to produce our winter food, so we helped weed and water. We knew bees made honey, milk came from the cows in the pasture when we brought them into the barn, and the chickens laid the eggs we gathered. We collected rocks and feathers, made mud pies, and took hikes in the pasture. We learned what different weeds were, the names of trees, and how to milk a cow. We watched the weather by the clouds in the sky and for the dark side of the moon and the full moon. These were all life lessons that shaped us into the adults we became. We found a balance in life that I fear is becoming more difficult to find, unless we are mindful of our great need for it.

TODAY I LIVE SIMPLY AND QUIETLY IN THE WOODS WITH nature surrounding me — it is my healing place. My thoughts still go deep as I continue to learn each day. I enjoy nurturing with nature. When I feel depressed, it is nature that alters my state of mind and helps me feel whole again, as does the practice of living with an *attitude of gratitude*. I am a naturalist, an earth keeper, medicine maker, gardener, needlewoman, pine needle basket maker, a granny woman and teacher, to name a few roles, and I continue to make plant medicine.

In my woodland home, there are windows on all sides that look into the woods, and I have become mindful of looking out a window whenever I pass by. I sometimes stop for a minute or two and am pleasantly surprised at what I call a *quick nature fix*. I have seen grass and weeds move and soon a turtle emerges. While standing at my kitchen sink, I casually glance out the window as a barred owl lands in one of the trees close to the house. I think to myself that she is watching the meadow for food for her babies. Another time I might see a mama deer with her two fawns walk out from the trees or see a bird with dried grass in its mouth land to sit on my open back porch, and I know a nest is being made in an old birdhouse sitting on a bench. Living in the country I might see more wildlife, but I have lived in town also, and on a daily walk have found a feather in my path, a walnut or hedge apple that fell from the tree above or a wildflower blooming along the walkway. I am always looking, always seeing, always finding treasures of nature.

WHEN THE MALAISE OF LIVING IN THIS CHAOTIC WORLD begins to get the best of me, I know it is time to be in nature again. A simple walk to the mailbox down my long country lane is enough to turn my thoughts around, and I often pick a bouquet of grasses and wildflowers along the way, or discover wild hops vining into the tree.

I listen to the wind rustling in the trees above and find answers where there were none before. I ask the lavender plant for a flower from her lovely plant body to soothe my soul, which she graciously gives, and I give her a strand of my hair to thank her. I spent many sleepless nights listening to the owls hooting outside my window as I was waffling about whether to write a book or not. When I would sit in my garden on a full moon night or fix a glass of iced lemon balm drink on a hot summer day, I would hear the spirits around me telling me *go ahead – follow your broken and heavy heart – and do it.*

Finally, the book began to write itself – almost. After years of writing newsletters for my shops, positive responses and emails from people saying I needed to write more or write a book, I listened and took it to heart. I thank ALL OF YOU who uplifted me along the way and planted the seed in my heart to write this book.

We do not have to walk in space or on water
to experience a miracle;
The real miracle is to be awake in the present moment.
Walking on the green Earth,
we realize the wonder of being alive.
-Thich Nhat Hanh

AUTHOR'S NOTE

HOW TO READ THIS BOOK

Each season has its own wonder, its own special place and a
purpose in the pattern of creation.
- Cicero

*O*ur lives revolve around the seasons. I love living in the midwest and celebrating the seasons of Mother Earth by living in Spring, Summer, Autumn and Winter.

Our lives have seasons too — the Learning, Earning, and Yearning years. We are defined by being children, adolescents, adults, middle aged, or old.

The seasons of life are further delineated by the months of the year: March, April and May being Spring; June, July and August are Summer; Autumn's September, October and November; and the Winter months of December, January and February. We live life fully by living in the moment as the months become the seasons of our life, and too soon the years of our life on Mother Earth are over.

THIS IS A BOOK THAT IS MEANT TO BE READ A MONTH AT a time — in the current month you pick the book up to read. And then, keep the book handy and read it at the beginning of each month. My desire is that it will inspire all to find joy and blessings in each and every month. If you would like to go further, use a notecard and jot down your blessings in nature you observe each month and record them before you begin the next month's chapter. Writing gives us pause to think about what inspires us — to learn about the big old tree in the backyard, or about the bird that is building a nest in it, or the plant that appears in our pathway and what it really means. It is interesting to find information about what grows close to where we live.

I find joy everywhere — in a flower and leaves to press for note-cards or making jelly from Queen Anne's lace flowers that bloom profusely nearby, picking elderberries or a simple walk and finding a feather in my path.

My desire is that by the end of the year and the end of the book, after reading the 12 months one month at a time, you will find a serenity and quietness in your life from Nature as I have. I hope this book becomes a meditation between you and Mother Earth. Follow the months and re-read each year as you *learn, see* or *feel* something not noticed before. Each month of the year is a celebration, and I encourage you to look around at what lives nearby, what is blooming or producing fruit now, or simply listen to the wind in the trees above. It is a ritual and celebration to live fully and mindfully each month and season.

> *Touch the earth, love the earth, honor the earth,*
> *her plains, her valleys, her hills and her seasons:*
> *Rest your spirit in her solitary places.*
> -Henry Beston (1888-1968)

I AM AN ORDINARY PERSON LIVING AN ORDINARY LIFE

enriched by the extraordinary creatures, plants and trees of nature and Mother Earth around me. I have been a lifelong learner continuing to ask why and how. I have honored the process and give gratitude for it.

So, I share my thoughts and musings with you. This book was written from my heartfelt love of living close to the land. I ask your help in protecting Mother Earth for generations to come.

Earth Blessings, *Twila*

NOTE: THIS BOOK REFLECTS MY OWN PERSONAL thoughts, ideas and opinions. When using herbs, the traditional or personal uses are stated.

Disclaimer: *Do not consume any plant as food or medicine until absolutely sure of its identification. Also, consult a professional health care provider before taking any medicinal herb.*

Caution: *For any wild plant that is collected in the wild, be sure to know what you are picking and eating. There are often poisonous look-alike plants. With a little practice, you will know for sure which plant is which. Do not taste anything until you know for sure what it is and that it has not been sprayed. It is easy to learn this. Take a weed walk with a qualified person, ask questions, and read a plant identification book. Be sure.*

THANK YOU

I DEDICATE this book to my late husband Dave, my life partner, who supported every idea I came up with and loved me through them.

- To my dear children, Tamara and Daniel, who inspire me every day and are always there for me. Loving thanks to Tamara for helping pull the book together and into a reality.

- To my grandchildren, Devin and Tyler and Dylan and Tobin, who inspire me to keep teaching the lessons of life.

- To my dear mom, Verneeda, and Grandmother Lydia, who taught me about life, and to the ancestral grandmothers who taught them, so the knowledge could be passed on through the generations.

- To my father, who taught me about the weather and what I call *earth-notes*.

- To my sweet friends, for your continued encouragement and friendship.

- And to all my relations, the plants and creatures who inhabit the earth we all walk together.

January

)

THE VIEW FROM MY WINDOW

Each year is a fresh beginning,
A brand new undertaking...
New friends to know, new ways to go
In the life that we are making.
-Unknown

New beginnings, a gray day, and cold wind blowing describe my New Year's Day. I am cozy inside as I sit near the hearth drinking a cup of hot herbal tea. It looks like winter outside my window today – and indeed it is winter. The stillness of January that comes with the falling snow brings serenity to my life. It is a time to find balance. The heavy snow brings the country to a standstill – at least long enough to enjoy the white sugar-like coating on the trees and bushes.

I am in awe of Mother Nature, and this time of year especially so, with the beautiful pictures she creates in the landscape. Snow crystal diamond dust is tossed all around the outside of my home and sparkles when the sun shines. And after the grayness, once again the sun shines and melts the snow, giving the earth a drink of life to the roots hidden below the surface fast asleep. The miniature crystal snowflakes, of which scientists say no two are alike, are formed around a speck of dust and add nutrients when the snow melts, building up the soil I will plant my seeds in when spring arrives.

Let it snow –
Nature is full of genius, full of divinity;
So that not a snowflake escapes its fashioning hand.
-Thoreau

I need to be in Nature or close to it. My senses and soul come alive with the sounds of wildness. I am a lover of all things wild – especially birds. Offered a trip to a faraway place or a walk in my woods, I would choose the walk in my woods, or in a park, or by a lake every single time. There is beauty to be found every month of the year wherever we are. Some months I need to look a little longer and deeper to find it, and then, be still a moment to enjoy and appreciate it.

There is nothing in the world more beautiful
than the forest clothed to its very hollows in snow.
It is the still ecstasy of nature, wherein every spray,
every blade of grass, every spire of reed,
every intricacy of twig, is clad in radiance.
-William Sharp

I love living in the Midwest where we experience the seasons and changes they bring, but January can sometimes test me. The cold frigid temperatures and the forlorn gray skies of January days feel as though they will go on forever. These are the "dark days of winter," when the nights seem darker and longer, even though the days have been gradually lengthening since Solstice. I spend a lot of the winter days at home reading or working on projects. It is a perfect time to contemplate and honor the month of January. The winter days are a gift, and I feel the need to wrap myself around them.

Winter is a time for comfort, for good food and warmth;
for the touch of a friendly hand, and for talk beside the fire:
it is the time for home.
-Edith Stilwell

I am inspired to finish old projects now and to start new ones. I take time to sit by the fire stitching on needlework or reading a book while the soup pot simmers on the stove. January is a time to pull inward – to hibernate and find more balance in life, to contemplate on the year past and the new year beginning.

Perhaps I am a bear,
or some other hibernating animal underneath,
for the instinct to be half asleep all winter is so strong in me.
-Anne Lindbergh

The cold January wind blows around the outside corners of my home, and the bare branches of the trees are moaning and groaning. Soon I hear sleet pelting the windows, and then the snow comes, making it treacherous to walk outside. I imagine all living things outdoors have found a place to hunker down – perhaps under the heavy cedar tree branches or in a hollow of a tree. The birds were well fed before the snowstorm arrived, and they will feast happily when the storm passes, scratching to uncover the seeds in the feeders. And when I awaken in the morning there will be another layer of snow upon the brown ground like white frosting on a chocolate cake.

The north wind doth blow, and we shall have snow.
-English nursery rhyme

And then the weather changes again. For a few days in January we will experience what is called the "January thaw," with temperatures climbing to the 50's, and the earth will begin to thaw and heave for a few days. After a taste of what spring must feel like, January comes roaring back with bone-chilling cold.

It is a customary ritual for me at bedtime after the lights are shut off to look out the big window into the woods. When my eyes become accustomed to the darkness, I can see beyond the split rail fence into the trees that are perfectly etched on the landscape. The almost full and brilliant moon is reflecting off the newly fallen snow, enticing and calling me to come for a walk to see what is beyond. It is tempting, but my older "voice of reason" and night-gown clad body say, *not now*. Instead, I stare into the eerie stillness of an almost-light and almost-dark night. And in the morning I reverse the ritual.

My morning ritual begins gazing out the big window again to greet the day. I am an early morning riser, loving the dark early hours with the surrounding quietness, enjoying a hot cup of herbal tea while waiting and watching for the dawn to greet me. I light a candle and sit in my comfortable wingback chair close to the big window and gaze out at the still-nighttime sky. I listen to the wind move through the treetops, knowing my little feathered friends are still asleep, sheltered in the sanctuary of the red cedar tree branches along the fence row beyond.

My resident hoot owl likes to roost in the big old sycamore tree and hoots to let me know he is awake also, and he sees me in my little home with only the very dim light of the candle. He is hooting away as if to say, *what are you doing up at this hour?* I feel he is watching over his kingdom and mine too, and telling me all is right in the world. I never tire of listening to the owls, and there are many of them living in my woods. The barred owls fly in and out of the trees, and it is comforting to know they find my woods peaceful too. Many times as they communicate with their jabber-ing, monkey-like talk, I open my window quietly to eavesdrop more closely on their conversation. The window does not stay open for long, as the cold wind is chilling the room. I have read in folklore that seeing an owl or hearing an owl can mean bad luck or death, but I have never believed that to be true. I believe owls are teachers of wisdom.

It is a wonderful time to think about my day ahead, to rejoice and be glad in it, knowing I cannot fix all the troubles in the world but can find peace where I am. These are simple pleasures to be found in my little home in the woods and in my own little corner of the world.

I love Judith Duerk's words in her book, *Circle of Stones,* about winter coming around full circle – about our fatigue, feeling our age and the aches in our bones, and wanting to reconnect with the dark energy of winter in our roots. She writes beautifully about the darkness of winter. I feel those words as I greet the January dawn.

I think of many things in the early morning, but mostly nothing important. Resting quietly in the darkness is the way I like to start the first hour of a January morning. In the wee hours I depart from my bed and find the house colder than normal and know a bitter cold day lies ahead. Temperatures last night were at 10 degrees and wind chills much colder. I know my morning duties will be scooping a path to the five bird feeders, filling them with bird food, and adding water to the heated birdbath. Food and water are important to my little feathered friends, and there will be many birds visiting the feeders today. As soon as I am done with my "bird duties" and close the door behind me, I look back and see four fluffed-up bluebirds appearing at the birdbath, drinking away with their heads bobbing up and down as if to say, *Thank you.*

On a bitter cold winter morning, my favorite little bird to watch is the downy woodpecker. The suet feeder hangs on the side of the arbor close to my big window, so I have a good view. He nods his head to and fro as if to see me better, but I know he is really surveying the area around him. His tuxedo color of black and white feathers with a splash of red on his head is very fashionable on this winter morning – the exact colors I would choose for a winter outing myself. He is enjoying his morning breakfast and soon another joins him, and then a flicker joins the party. The downy is one bird I can always count on to show up at the feeder. Watching the birds is an enjoyable pastime on winter days, and I am glad the birdfeeding station is close to my window where I can watch their daily bird antics.

I count six cardinals dressed in showy bright red feathers enjoying the specialty seed I put out for them. The goldfinch feeder holds thirty of the little yellow and black birds when the thistle seed is freshly filled to the top. And since I filled it late yesterday afternoon, they are clustered on every available perch with several finches "waiting in the wings" for their place to eat.

It is January and I am still seeing robins. The heated birdbath hosted eight robins at once the other day, and they seemed most appreciative of the warm water and drink here often. When I was growing up the robins went south for the winter, and we would impatiently await their arrival in the spring, but now the robins winter over here in the Midwest – a sign of global warming, I fear.

It is January and the Canadian geese are still here, and they look hard to find open water that has not frozen over yet. The watershed lake has been home to many geese – sometimes so full of geese that the lake looks black. But it will eventually freeze completely over and the geese will move on, finding a bigger lake. I love the honking that announces their arrival, and I hurry out to the porch and watch them flying low. They circle around the lake, looking for a perfect spot to land for the night, as well as checking it out to make sure they will be safe. I think how sad it would be not to see or hear these big birds of the wild flying in their distinctive V-pattern formation. I worry about the changing of global patterns and know many of the species of animals and birds are on the endangered list due to fewer protected areas for them to survive, as well as the issues of chemical pesticides being used abundantly.

In the Midwest, the concern has been over the prairie chicken. In the last survey there were 84% fewer seen, yet the "powers that be" do not yet list them endangered. If we cannot protect our wild friends from extinction, how do we prevent it for ourselves? I offer a prayer to the Universe and our ancestors to watch over us all.

The winter sunsets in the Midwest are some of the most beautiful and breathtakingly spectacular in the world, according to a world survey in 2015. I can see the bright colors of the sunset as I look through the dark gray silhouettes of the trees in my woods while standing on my front porch. As I think about going back into the house, the sunset changes and is even more beautiful than a moment before. I marvel at Mother Nature's paintbrush and the scenes she creates. Pictures never do a sunset justice, but I grab my camera anyway and try to capture the glorious view. It is a simple country blessing to look through the trees to the sunset on a cold winter early evening.

A WINTER JANUARY DAY IS A GOOD TIME TO MAKE HERB-infused oils for salves and ointments. I grow my own plants in my garden in the summer and then harvest and dry for use later on. I begin my infused oil on a new moon, let it set for two full moons (about 6 weeks), and then decant on the full moon. I consider the full moon to be the night of the full moon, as well as the night before and the night after. I want the infusion to go through at least one full moon cycle or more, absorbing the energy from the plants and from the moon. My infusion sits in a dark cupboard, away from heat and light until the full moon appears, and then I sit it on my windowsill for the three nights only of the full moon. The infusion will absorb the strong moonbeam rays and energy that strengthens my homemade medicine. The jars sitting in the moon-light on a wide windowsill are pretty as a picture, and I know they will be good for healing. The next full moon I will decant and make my salve and medicine.

MY NEW YEAR'S DAY RITUAL EACH year is to start paperwhites (Narcissus flowers), "planting" a few bulbs in a jar with pebbles and water. Three weeks later, more or less, I have blooming fragrant flowers on the kitchen table, giving forth spring green color and blossoms that are as white as the January snow.

I clean out the freezer and find the frozen rhubarb, raspberries and strawberries. January is a good time to make jam from frozen fruits I gathered last summer. The frozen elderberry heads will make more elderberry syrup.

The seed catalogs have arrived, and on a Sunday afternoon in front of a warm fire, I sit with my paper and pen and make a list of what I would like to plant and add to my vegetable garden, and the seeds I want to plant in the flower and herb patch. When I am done going through the seed catalogs, I pass them on to friends so they can spend a winter afternoon going through them and daydreaming about their spring gardening.

January days and January nights are the perfect time to do what we really want to do, especially watching the birds feed at the feeders, gazing at the full moon, or at a morning sunrise or evening sunset, reading a new book, learning a new craft, writing in a gratitude journal, starting paperwhite bulbs – the list is endless and rewarding.

Winter, a lingering season,
it is a time to gather golden moments,
embark upon a sentimental journey, and enjoy every idle hour.
-John Boswell

So, we find time in January to appreciate winter and nurture ourselves. We honor the winter month of January, and my New Year's wish to all is this:

May the sun bring you new energy by day,
May the moon softly restore you by night,
May the rain wash away your worries,
May the wind blow new strength into your being,
And may you walk gently through the world
and know the beauty of the days of your life.
-Apache blessing

THE JANUARY FULL MOON

As the Sun kisses the earth good night,
The Moon appears with her radiant light.
-Unknown

I hear the coyotes howling outside my home in the woods close by. They form their circle and yip and howl with each other – and why not, it is a full moon.

I have always been intrigued by the full moon, the energy it gives forth, and the mystery and history of it. My plant medicines are made with the moon phases, and I plant my garden and harvest it with the phases of the moon. Many of us believe the energy and gravitational pull of the moon to the Earth makes the plants grow better at certain times, and I believe it makes my plant medicine stronger too.

It is well documented that the moon affects the tides, people's state of mind, and the germination and growing of seeds. I find it interesting to learn about the waxing and waning moons and everything in-between, but most of all about the full moon and the names used for them throughout history.

Native Americans and early settlers named the moons as a method of keeping track of the seasons and the months. I can envision a time when families would sit in front of the fire and elders would tell the stories of the moon – stories to be passed down to the next generation.

Names given to the full moons were to identify the time of year, and many times there was more than one name for a month's particular moon – depending on tribe, locality or region. From this they could plan their planting, hunting and harvesting.

The January full moon is *Wolf Moon*. This moon appeared when the wolves howled in hunger outside the villages, as it was more difficult for wolves (and people) to find food in the cold and deep snows of January. This full moon is also known as *Cold Moon, Moon After Yule, Very Cold Moon, Cold Makes the Trees Crack Moon*, and *Cold Night Moon*. In our locality, the tribe of Osage Indians called it the *Moon Stands Alone Moon*.

Each month I observe the full moon, and in January I am looking through my big south window on a cold and forlorn night, the earth covered in white, reflecting the full light of the moon on the snow. I ponder the names given to this particular moon, and I want to break into song at its beauty, its light and its strength.

THE WINTER GARDEN

*Anyone who thinks gardening begins in the spring and ends in
the fall is missing the best part of the year -
for gardening begins in January with the dream.*
-Josephine Nuese

In January there is much to do, and perhaps daydreaming is the best of all things to do. The seed catalogs arrive in my mailbox and I become lost within the pages as I plan what I want to plant in the coming springtime.

The ground is cold and frozen in January, but I know it is alive underneath the blanket of snow that insulates the roots deep in the earth. And above the ground, remnants of summer and autumn remain. I see color and texture creating a landscape that is interesting to look at throughout the winter months.

As I plan a new garden area at my Kansas home, I look for shrubs and plants that give winter appeal. I like creating layers in the garden that make for a pretty picture in January when there is no snow on the ground – and perhaps more importantly *with* snow on the ground. In my last garden I learned what I liked best in January in my yard, so I will duplicate some of that in my new garden.

I like leaving the fronds of asparagus; although they are brown in January, their "to and fro" movement in the wind is hypnotic to watch. The seedpods left on the black-eyed Susans, the poppies, and anything that has pods or berries still remaining create an interesting winter landscape, as well as providing food for the birds. The yellow and red twig dogwood shrubs are especially pretty in the winter months, and I clip a few red stalks to create a winter vignette beside my front door. The clumping birch with its peeling bark and the corkscrew willow create more texture as well. Some of the more dense shrubs hold the cottony tufts of snow to add to the wintery picture. And an evergreen tree such as a spruce or pine, or the prairie cedar, is pretty in all seasons, especially in the brown-gray landscape of winter. The common prairie tree I am most fond of is the wild red cedar (*Juniperus virginiana*). It seeds prolifically, to the disdain of many, but I admire it for its tenacity and strength through the coldest days of a January winter. The native Red Cedar is also called *Sanctuary Tree*, as it gives shelter to small animals and bird friends during the bitter cold winter days.

The holly shrub is another favorite and is mainly thought of as something to decorate with at the holidays, but with its dark shiny green leaves and bright red berries, its beauty is exceptional when the snow accumulates at its feet. I will remember to plant the two required for berries in my new yard.

I enjoy gazing out my big window on a snowy winter January day with an interesting view – color as well as texture – not only in my yard but also the layers of hills that lie beyond.

There is something infinitely healing
in the repeated refrains of nature –
the assurance that dawn comes after night,
and spring after winter.
-Rachel Carson

IN THE KITCHEN IN JANUARY

⚜

he winter months are for making soup – a perfect comfort food that is nutritious and warms from the inside out. I find soups generally easy and satisfying to make. As with all things I make, I add my good intentions, blessing the food with love. When cooking with my grandsons, I would hold my hands above the food as in prayer and softly voice my love and intent. My grandsons would call this "grandma's secret ingredient – LOVE." They said it made the food taste so much better, and I agree.

WINTER BEAN SOUP
1 large onion, chopped
1 clove garlic, diced
1 qt. chicken broth
1 qt. (approx.) home canned tomatoes or 1 large can tomatoes, chopped in food processor
2 cans black beans, rinsed and drained
1 small can (15 oz.) aduki beans (or pinto)
1 T. Worcestershire sauce
1/2 c. mild salsa
Salt and pepper to taste
1 T. dried thyme

1 T. herb blend (recipe follows)
Optional: 1-2 tsp. chili powder for added flavor
Optional: 3 slices dried astragalus root slices

Brown onion and garlic in coconut oil. Add broth. Add tomatoes that have been put in food processor so there are no large chunks. Add rest of ingredients and bring to a strong simmer (not boil) and turn off burner to let set for 1-2 hours covered for flavors to blend through. Reheat and serve.

Note: *The dried sliced astragalus root can be purchased at a health food store – traditionally it is used to boost the immune system. I use it every time I make any soup during colds/flu season. Remove the pieces before serving soup and throw away, making sure no splinters came off (can be put into a muslin bag before adding to soup for easy retrieval).* I have also added leftover potatoes, browned ground beef, or diced chicken to this soup.

WILD RICE AND CHICKEN SOUP
2 – 2 ½ c. chopped or shredded cooked chicken
1 medium onion, diced
2 stalks celery, diced
2 medium carrots, coarsely shredded
1 can condensed cream of chicken soup (approx. 10-11 oz)
5 c. chicken broth
5 c. water
1 T. thyme (in addition to the herb blend)
1 T. herb blend (recipe follows) or more to taste as soup cooks
Rice: Cook 2 c. wild rice, according to package (I cook rice ahead of time).

Method: Sauté the celery and onion until translucent. Add rest of ingredients, including rice. Cover and simmer (no bubbles) for 1 hour or until carrots are cooked through. Delicious.

ALL-PURPOSE HERB BLEND

1 T. dried basil
1 T. dried thyme
1 T. oregano
1 tsp. rosemary powder
½ tsp. black pepper
½ tsp. onion powder
½ tsp. garlic powder

Use by teaspoon or tablespoon for soups. I use this to sprinkle on roasted veggies, chicken baked in oven, to make herbed butter, add to biscuit dough, etc., and I use this in place of salt.

ONION CHEESE BALL
A favorite recipe from Sue H.

We love this and find it is better made ahead and refrigerated for a day or two for the flavors to pull through. *(The jar of onion/garlic jam can be found at kitchen stores with a brand name of Stonewall Kitchen)*

1/3 c. Roasted onion/garlic jam
1/4 tsp. ground sage, optional
2 – 8oz. cream cheese blocks, softened
1 ½ c. Monterey Jack cheese, shredded
Pecans, crushed to roll ball in

Refrigerate 3 hours, then form into 2 small balls or one large ball, roll in crushed pecans to coat, arrange on plate, cover and refrigerate one day before serving for flavors to meld. Serve with crackers. Delicious.

CHIPPED BEEF DIP
Make this ahead of time and put in oven 30 minutes before serving. (Good for a group, from neighbor Sue W.)

8 oz. cream cheese
8 oz. sour cream
1/4 c. finely chopped onion
1/4 tsp. garlic powder
3 oz. (approx.) of dried chipped beef, cut up

Mix all together, top with 2 T. melted butter and some chopped walnuts. Bake 30 minutes at 350 degrees. Serve with snack crackers.

SNOW DAYS MIX
All ages love this!
3 c. Rice Chex
2 c. Corn Chex
1 c. small pretzel twists
1 c. honey roasted peanuts
2 – 12 oz. pkg. white baking chips
1 – 12 oz. pkg. M&M's chocolate or mint flavored

Melt baking chips (only) according to directions. Pour melted white chocolate over cereals, pretzels and peanuts. Stir gently. Spread on parchment paper. Sprinkle with the M&M's. Cool 1 hour. Break into pieces when cooled.
Note: *Ingredients can be changed somewhat to suit your own taste.*

JANUARY ACTIVITIES WITH CHILDREN

When the kids are home from school on a snow day, it is fun to have a project or two lined up for them to do – and something to eat, as they are always hungry.

My grandsons loved doing these projects when they were small. I would keep a file on fun things to do, and when I visited them or they visited me, we would have fun and make memories.

These are "kid-tested" ideas they enjoyed doing. (Remember if working with heat or scissors to supervise closely).

TORTILLA SNOWFLAKES
Need:
8-inch flour tortillas at room temperature
Children's scissors or adult scissors with supervision
Cookie sheet lined with parchment paper
Melted butter to brush on
Cinnamon sugar

Method: Gently fold the tortilla in halves or fourths depending on age of child (fourths work well). Cut out a simple snowflake pattern into the tortilla as one would do with a piece of paper – keep it simple so tortilla won't fall apart. Lay the tortilla snowflake on parchment paper on a cookie sheet, brush with melted butter, and sprinkle with cinnamon sugar. Bake at 350 degrees for 5 minutes or less (watch for browning, as you don't need to brown them, just crisp them). Remove from oven, cool a bit and ready to eat. Children love the novelty of this idea and the snowflakes are delicious too!

PRETZEL CANDY
Need:
Rollo brand candies
Waffle shaped square pretzels or small pretzels
Parchment lined cookie sheet

Method: Unwrap individual Rollo Candies and put one candy on each pretzel. Place in oven at 250 degrees for a minute or two until the candy looks "shiny." Remove from oven and carefully put another pretzel on top of the melted candy (remember the cookie sheet is hot, so you could slide the pretzels off to a flat surface making it easier for kids to work on). This makes a pretzel candy "sandwich."
Note: Another version we like is omitting the top pretzel and putting a half pecan on top to create "turtle candy." These are fun to make for a New Year's party too.

ANTIQUE WHITE IRONSTONE

I collect antique ironstone – white as the January snow. I have a big shelf full of white ironstone in an old cupboard, and it all started with a simple little cream pitcher I remembered a long time ago in Grandma's kitchen.

I do not have Grandma's little ironstone cream pitcher today – in fact, I have no idea what happened to it now that grandma is gone. Even though I don't have Grandma's pitcher, I do have another little ironstone pitcher that reminds me of Grandma and my memories of years gone by. I also have a big ironstone pitcher, an ironstone coffeepot, sugar container, butter pats, small dishes and platters, large and small, and more. I am smitten and unabashedly in love with this simple look of plain white ironstone.

Ironstone came into the marketplace around the mid-19th century and was used as everyday dishes at that time. I am not sure how safe they might be for food today, so I use them more decoratively now. A big white ironstone platter makes a nice base for a vignette of small vases of flowers, or for a nest with twigs and berries, or old pincushions to rest upon.

And the little cream pitcher like grandma used to have? Instead of putting cream in it I use it as a small vase for flowers all year long, buying a small bouquet of flowers at the supermarket in the winter when I cannot pick them from my own garden. Grandma would approve, as she loved her little white ironstone pitcher – and her flowers too.

WOODEN BOWLS

*J*t is January, and a big wooden bowl holds a collection of old handmade mittens, and another I use for the seed catalogs as they arrive, and yet another one holds my current knitting project.

I started collecting old wooden handmade bowls many years ago, and today I use them for a variety of purposes.

I have been asked, "What constitutes a collection?" Normally one might have more than two and call it a collection or maybe a dozen, but a collection of several dozen might be called a *super collection* (or the collector might be called a hoarder). I am guilty of collecting many wooden bowls, and I am not sure I could offer an explanation as to why I collect them. I look at an old bowl and it speaks to me. I can close my eyes and see a grandmother mixing up cookies for her grandchildren in that old bowl long ago, or see apples in the bowl after being picked off the old apple tree in the backyard orchard, or see bread dough rising or green beans from the garden filling it. Old wooden bowls were used constantly, and some are worse for the wear. But the wear is the patina and history that makes them so appealing. I wonder whose hands lovingly

34

made this bowl from the wood of a fallen tree so long ago and whose hands held the bowl while mixing up supper?

My collection has spanned twenty-five years, and I have gradually narrowed the collection down due to necessity when I moved – I did not have space for all of them.

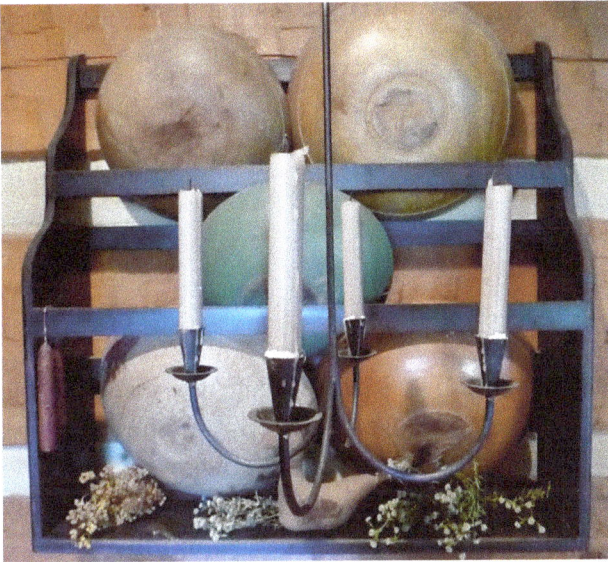

It is January, a new year, and I count how many bowls I now have in my collection. There are fifteen residing on bowl racks, a few in a corner cupboard and various other places in my home. Many of them are used in some way, holding something. There is always one sitting on my kitchen island. I love the big old painted bowl that sits a little lopsided from the wood drying out for over a hundred years of time, and I find that nothing completes the simple warm look I love better than a big wooden bowl in the middle of my old farm table.

I ALWAYS LEAVE ONE BOWL PURPOSEFULLY EMPTY TO receive the blessings of the day.

STITCHES IN TIME

❦

A STITCH HERE AND A STITCH THERE, AND SOON A PROJECT IS DONE.

*J*anuary is a perfect time for needle and thread. Needlework has always been an interest of mine. However, it was more the admiration for it than the actual "doing" of it. My maternal grandmother and my mother were quilters, and I tried my hand at it thinking it would be genetic and I would follow in their footsteps. Not to be.

Feather Stitch

As an antiques dealer and lover of old things, I started my own collection of beautiful old handmade quilts – some with patriotic themes done in red, white and blue, some were made with the heart motif, a few were friendship quilts with many names stitched on them, and some were what I called "country quilts," made from many pieces of fabric, including some from old feed sacks. The patterns were intriguing, as were their names: *Drunkard's Path, Bowtie, Windmill, Tumbling Blocks, Log Cabin* and many more.

Finding a unique *crazy quilt* with the cloth sugar sacks being used as backing and the word "sugar" clearly seen was especially rewarding. The exquisite and different colored stitches on crazy quilts were endearing, and I would often find a name and a date stitched into the quilt, which added to the excitement.

When my collection became *more* than a collection I began selling quilts through my shop and antique shows. I still kept the quilts that tugged at my heart – oh, the stories these quilts could tell if they could only talk. I know the stitches represent happiness, sadness, loneliness and more.

Today, twenty- five years later, I am a woman who loves to stitch. My stitching on cloth is different, as I use wool in rug hooking and now hand appliqué, sometimes using what is called the *blanket stitch*, but mostly I like using the *blind stitch*, letting the wool take center stage. I dye my own wool, change designs to suit my tastes, choose colors and color plan, and then the stitching begins. It could be a hundred or a thousand or more stitches, depending on the size of the project. I have stitched in happiness, in grief, in loneliness and times in between – whether with wool for rug hooking or with thread in appliqué – many stitches in time and through the years. I understand how stitches get women through tough times as well as happy times, and why each quilt or stitching project is deeply meaningful.

Research now tells us that it relieves stress to stitch, whether knitting, quilting, crocheting, rug hooking or appliqué. Researchers tell us what women through the ages have always known – that stitching is meditative, hobbies engage the imagination and help keep our brains active, and working on a project is relaxing. It helps the brain to learn new skills like figuring out a pattern, and then making it into something very special, which also boosts our confidence.

A women's stitching group is necessary in my life. When I moved, I left behind an active wool group where members either rug hooked or wool appliquéd. Being within the group played an important part in our lives.

When I moved to Kansas, it was hard to find people to stitch with, to visit with, to exchange ideas and recipes with. I missed the friendship and camaraderie, and I knew being with others and sharing, laughing and crying too, was vital to my health and well-being, and more so as I age.

I started my own stitching group by word-of-mouth. I asked people I had met who seemed like-minded to join me once a month. Six attended that first gathering, and now we number close to twenty, with an average of twelve or more attending each monthly get-together. Close friendships are formed within stitching group. There is time for visiting, snacking and of course, needlework. The group's interests vary within the needle and thread framework – some knit, others crochet, hand piece quilts, beadwork with needle and thread, and wool appliqué. When someone needs help with a knit stitch or wants to learn to crochet, someone else in the group will lend a helping hand. We love seeing each other each month, and this group is something we all look forward to. It has become a very special group of women who enjoy coming together to stitch and connect.

I have done a lot of stitching projects through the years and continue to do so. Sometimes I am asked what I will do with all the things I have made. My answer, with a smile, is simply this: *It is not my worry, as I am here to enjoy the journey along the way – a stitch at a time.*

Antique crazy quilt block, personalized by me with names and dates of women in my lineage.

GRATITUDE

It is not the joy that makes us grateful;
It is the gratitude that makes us joyful.
-David Steindl-Rast, Benedictine monk

THE JOURNAL

As each new year begins, it is like an empty bowl or basket that is ready to be filled up with good things – the happy moments of each day. It can change our lives when we adopt a spirit of gratitude, and this has taught me to be gentle with myself and others. I find myself listening more and being aware of the messages from the Universe. Keeping a gratitude journal helps me become more connected to life around me, to be mindful, and provides a way to recognize and remember my blessings.

I used to do the "rule of five," which was listing five things I was grateful for during that day. It could be as simple as *watching a red cardinal at the bird feeder*, or *taking an hour to sit in front of the fireplace on a cold snowy day and reading a good book*, or it could be more specific, like recording the name of the book I just finished reading. I have found it easiest to write my gratitude thoughts when retiring in the evening just before turning off the lamp, as my journal is sitting on a chest next to my bed. It has become part of my evening ritual. I list three to five things each evening in my gratitude journal. Doing so helps me keep an "Attitude of Gratitude" in my life.

THE JAR

A friend of mine had an alternative to the gratitude journal that I like and have used, and that is to keep a *Gratitude Jar*. I used a half gallon antique blue canning jar and set it at the back corner of my kitchen counter (no lid), and before I shut off the light and leave the kitchen at night, I write down ONE THING that I am most grateful for that day. (I have a pen and slips of paper handy in the under-counter drawer). This works well for me, and during times I am not doing a journal I will use the jar gratitude method. And the following New Year's Eve or New Year's Day, I take out the slips of paper and read the 365 daily gratitudes of the year just past. This has become an uplifting and inspiring way to begin another New Year ahead.

February

THE VIEW FROM MY WINDOW

If you truly love nature you will find beauty everywhere.
-Vincent van Gogh

*L*ife is to be savored in all seasons, including winter, and February is the heart of wintertime in the Midwest. According to the weather forecaster, a winter storm is brewing in my corner of the world, and I keep that bit of information in the back of my mind as I check the cupboards and the firewood supply here at my home in the woods.

I fear our last few mild winter days have led me into a sense of false security, and a little confusion as to which season this really is. And like most everyone else, I love the mild days we are blessed with at times in the middle of February. The brown earth (instead of white) and not having to wear a heavy coat when I am out makes me want to think winter might really be over – but I should know better by now.

And then the storm arrives! The winds howl, the snow falls in big flakes to the earth, drifting into big marshmallow mounds, the temperature drops at dusk, and schools are closed tomorrow.

A blizzard is a beautiful thing.
As the drifts pile up, topping the picket fence,
I can see from the windows the meadow trimmed with silver.
-Gladys Taber

The day following the storm, snowdrifts are everywhere. I doubt I can get out my front door until I scoop a three-foot drift away. It is a serene and magical snowscape. The winds have quieted and the woods are still.

This is typical February weather in the Midwest. We know what to expect from weather forecasters telling us ahead of time to prepare for a big snowstorm or a very mild day. I think about the days before weather radar, when our ancestors needed to rely on their intuition, the cloud formations, and the changing darkness of the sky to know a storm was coming. A blizzard could and did happen within an hour's space of time, and one did not want to be caught unaware, as it could mean life or death. I am thankful today I can plan ahead to make sure the pantry is well-stocked to make a pot of soup when the roads are packed with snow and school is closed. I am most grateful to be tucked into my cozy little home in the woods with the fireplace burning brightly, safe and warm from the winter winds that blow, and I am ready to embrace another winter day.

The snow-laden cedars are providing protection for the animals and birds to survive the howling winter winds and bitter cold temperatures. Mother Nature gives the animals and birds extra insulation in the winter and the instinct to find shelter when the storm arrives. I look out my big window at the field of volunteer cedar trees creating a pretty view on this winter day, and I am thankful the trees are there to provide shelter for the little creatures.

The Snow is lying very deep.
My house is sheltered from the blast.
I hear each muffled step outside,

I hear each voice go past.
-from *Convention* by Agnes Lee (1841-1937)

I put out a new bird feeding station a few days ago to go along with the other four feeders, knowing a storm was coming. The feeders are full of food, as there is very little for a bird to find when the snow is deep. The birds love the heated birdbath and many have frequented it. The heated birdbath is for the birds, quite literally, but I was wondering why it was empty every early morning, after I filled it late afternoon the day before. The mystery is now solved! As I walked quietly to the big window early last evening to take a last glimpse of the beautiful sunset as it disappeared on the horizon, I saw instead seven deer in my yard, and one was drinking from the heated birdbath! I was quite surprised and suspect they were thinking the warm water was put there for them exclusively. I love seeing the deer coming up from the creek nearby in the winter. It was a serendipitous end to the day and an unexpected pleasure.

I AM UP EARLY, AND AGAIN MY MORNING (AND EVENING) ritual is to gaze outside my window to see what I might see. The winter landscape is illuminated by the moon as it descends in the western sky, making way for the sun to rise in the east. These are magical moments. I know city dwellers can see this too, but I believe it is magnified a hundred times in the country, when life seems to stand still. The barred owls hoot a lot right now, and I sit quietly listening to them talk with each other in their own owl language. I never tire of listening to their hoots and love knowing they are in my woods close by. The snow is over a foot deep now, and my herb plants are sleeping under the insulation of the snow as they wait for spring to arrive.

On many winter days I am homebound, sometimes by choice and sometimes not. I am thankful to be inside today. We all need time to "disconnect" from everything. These days are sacred to me. I take them slow and easy and catch up on little projects that need doing, such as going through stacks of old magazines. I save magazines I feel are just too good to throw away, but now these piles of magazines are getting my attention. I leaf through them to see if they attract me the way they did a few years ago. Several magazines I never part with, so they stack up in a cupboard behind closed doors. But then I wonder why I keep them? I am sure one day everything will be on the Internet, and magazines will no longer be impatiently watched for in the mailbox, but I love taking my leisurely time looking at the pictures and reading the articles in a magazine. It is a perfect time to sit with a cup of hot tea and figure out what made a magazine interesting enough to keep in the first place. And then, I will find a new home for them, giving the magazines to a retirement home or to someone else who will find them interesting.

Winter is the time of promise because there is so little to do –
or because you can now and then permit yourself
the luxury of thinking so.
–S. Crawford

I love the simple life, where less is more and we value the little things sometimes taken for granted. The world seems to be in a constant state of discontent, and peace is hard to find wherever one may be.

During these last few weeks of winter, I will savor the simplicity of doing with less, eating less, running errands less, so that I can live a life of simple blessings here in my country home in the winter woods.

I know well that happiness is in the little things.
–J. Ruskin

February is the month of hearts and Valentine's Day, and I love the thought of leaving a *heart-print* wherever one goes, in whatever one does, and in whomever one meets.

Lydia's Flowers Rug, 2001. Antique pattern.

THE FEBRUARY FULL MOON

Every now and then Valentine's Day can be celebrated with the full moon, making it an extra special day. I call the full moon in February the *Valentine Moon,* but from history we know it was known by other names.

Traditionally, the February full moon is called the *Full Hunger Moon.* Native American tribes and early settlers referred to this moon as the *Full Hunger Moon* since harsh winter weather conditions in their areas made hunting difficult. It was also called *Full Snow Moon* because the snowfall was usually the heaviest in the month of February, and it was the time of year blizzards were expected. Living on the prairie, they also called the full moon the *Ground Squirrels Run Moon.*

Folklore says to watch the moon the first two weeks of the month and it will predict the growing season of spring and summer. If the curve of the moon is up, like a smile, the weather will be unusually dry. If the moon curves in a downward fashion, then the rains will pour and the growing season will be quite wet. If there is a full moon between February 1st and 19th, the crops should be good.

The Snow Moon

Snow falls all day into the night
Snuggling the world in downy white.
Old Man Moon hides his face
Behind a curtain of winter's lace.
- From "When the Moon is Full" – a book for children by
Penny Pollack

IN THE GARDEN IN FEBRUARY

The plants are still sleeping as I plan for the spring ahead. I gaze out into the gardens and admire the tall grasses planted in clumps as they gently move with the wind. The grasses were planted for structure as well as winter interest.

Bleeding Hearts is an old-fashioned perennial plant that my grand-mother had in her garden. I think of the heart-shaped pink flowers "all in a row" on its bending stem and vow to plant one at the edge of the woods when spring comes. It likes a shady spot where it is cool and moist.

Rosemary for remembrance
Lavender for devotion
Myrtle for love
Ivy for friendship
Rose geranium for preference
Marjoram for blushes of joy and happiness
Sage for domestic virtue and immortality
Rosebuds for young love

LOVE TEA
3/4 c. rose petals (love)
1/4 c. lavender blossoms (devotion)
1/8 c. rosemary (remembrance)
1/8 c. hibiscus flowers (sexuality)

Mix all dried ingredients. Store in airtight container.
For tea, use 1 tsp. to 1 T. per cup hot water, steeping 5 minutes.

A FEW THOUGHTS...

WHILE EATING LOTS OF CITRUS DURING THE WINTER, I save the peels to use fresh or dried in a simmering pan on the stove. I add spices (cinnamon stick, allspice, cloves) to water with the peels for a delightful fragrance that will fill the air and lift my winter spirits.

IF ONE HAS CAT OR DOG FOOD, OR BUYS GRAINS IN BULK or uses wool fabric, the chance of having pantry moths is very likely (they come in with the food and feed on the wool). I make loosely woven cloth "envelopes" to hold dried herbs that act as insect deterrents such as: rue, tansy, wormwood, catmint or pennyroyal and lay them on shelves in cupboards and closets.

FEBRUARY IS A GOOD TIME OF YEAR TO ENJOY BROWSING through the many seed catalogs that have arrived in the mailbox and send off my orders. I especially enjoy looking through a catalog while sipping a cup of hot herbal tea and taking notes as I leaf through the pages. I make a list of plants I might like to add to the herb garden or flower garden or change around when spring arrives.

I USE UP THE HERB VINEGARS MADE LAST SUMMER AND also the dried herbs. Soon another crop of herbs will be ready to harvest once again.

IN THE KITCHEN IN FEBRUARY

F ebruary is a wonderful time to make herb blends to use all through the year. These mixes are very easy to make. I choose to make my own, as there are no extra ingredients, fillers or preservatives added to what I make. I store in an airtight container. The mixes make nice gifts packaged in small jars.

MY FAVORITE HERB BLENDS

ALL-PURPOSE HERB BLEND (SEE JANUARY CHAPTER)

RANCH DRESSING BLEND
1 T. parsley
1 tsp. each: dill weed and onion powder
1/2 tsp. each: garlic powder and salt
1/4 tsp. black pepper

Add desired amount to equal portions mayonnaise and milk.

TACO SEASONING

3 T. chili powder

2 T. onion powder

1 T. each: ground cumin, garlic powder, paprika, oregano, sugar

1-1/2 tsp. salt

Use desired amount (1-3 tsp.) per pound cooked ground beef.

HERBS DE PROVENCE

1 T. each thyme, basil, rosemary, tarragon, savory

1 tsp. each marjoram, oregano

1 tsp. lavender (optional)

1 bay leaf crushed

Makes 1/3 cup. Serving size in 1/4 teaspoon.

Mix with olive oil and brush on fish before baking, rub on turkey before roasting, or make into a salad dressing.

FEBRUARY ACTIVITIES

Winter snowed-in days can be hard on moms and grandmas, as well as the children – they love to have something to do. The following projects are ones I have enjoyed doing with my grandchildren in February as we celebrate the month.

RED PIPECLEANER HEARTS

Quick and easy to make, and the hearts can be glued to a card as a Valentine.

Take one pipe cleaner, plain red or sparkly red, fold in half so the folded end becomes the bottom point of the heart. With the two ends at the top, make a twisty end, and bend out two curved parts to finish making the heart.

HEART PUZZLE

This can work with most any design.

We draw a big heart, full size to fill a sheet of red construction paper, and in big letters print the words "I LOVE U" on two or three lines, then cut the heart in six or more different pieces, with either straight lines, scalloped, or zigzag lines and it becomes a heart puzzle. This can be put into an envelope and given to a friend for a Valentine wish. A puzzle could be made from a purchased Valentine card and then cut into pieces. We have had more fun making our own with different sayings.

VALENTINE TREAT

Grilled chocolate heart sandwich

Two bread slices with outer sides coated lightly with butter.

On the inside of the bread, put squares of milk chocolate candy bar.

With help from adult, toast in a skillet over low to medium heat until browned and chocolate is melted.

Dust with powdered sugar and cut out with large heart-shaped cookie cutter

Note: Raspberry jam, nuts, peanut butter or marshmallow cream, sliced bananas could be added. Yummy! Everyone loves this.

HEARTS FOR FEBRUARY

A loving heart is the truest wisdom.
-Charles Dickens

I keep a big old wooden bowl full of hearts on my table
this time of year. Many of the hearts I have purchased
and many are handmade from cloth, and a few have been gifts to

me, made with loving stitches. One of the hearts is a small antique carved wooden heart mold, another is a cinnamon heart, and yet another is a small cement heart, and two are rocks I have collected in the shape of a heart. My large antique wooden bowl overflows with hearts and always takes "center stage" in February on my table. It is a heart-warming collection in this month of hearts.

> *It matters not who you love,*
> *where you love, why you love,*
> *or how you love.*
> *It only matters that you love.*
> –John Lennon

LIGHTS IN THE WINDOW

We flew into the Harrisburg, Pennsylvania, airport on a cold February night quite a few years ago. In a rented car we drove to the Lancaster, Pennsylvania area. My first introduction to the Amish Pennsylvania Dutch area was the glow of candlelights in the windows of the homes.

I was enthralled by this ethereal view in the middle of the dark night in every home and wondered, *why do they put lights in the windows?* I fell in love with the area around Lancaster, as many do, and it mainly had to do with the welcoming little candlelights in the windows. I felt like I had come home.

After asking a few questions and doing a little research, I soon found answers about the candles in the windows. The historical viewpoint, it seems, comes from Ireland when in older times the church was outlawed and people could not get together to worship, but a traveling priest would see a candle in the window and know it was a safe haven, and he would be welcomed to say mass there. And now a Pennsylvania tradition tells travelers that when they see a light in the window, they can find shelter and hospitality if needed. What a wonderful way for the entire world to live, I think to myself, and wish a candle in the window could become a new-yet-old tradition in our homes today.

Many people now put a small electric candle light in the window to signal the year's end and to welcome in the New Year. Today, the lights in the window are always glowing in my home. I like to think of the lights as a welcoming gift to the neighborhood. It would be nice if every home had candlelights in the windows each evening at dark. I use my little lights as night lights in hallways and on cupboard shelves, as well as in my windows. The soft glow is always there to light the way.

Note: The lovely primitive-style electric candlelights can usually be purchased in country shops or online.

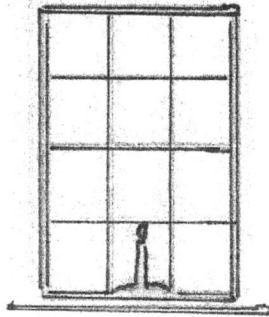

MY FEBRUARY BIRTHDAY

February is my birth month. I treasure each and every birthday, as they seem to come around more quickly now as I age. I have a few rituals I look forward to on my birthday each year.

My first ritual is this: For the last 35 years, as a birthday tradition and ritual, I send flowers to my mom on *MY* birth-day with a note of thanks for giving me this day. I order the flowers a week ahead of time to be delivered to her door, since we live in different states.

It is a simple pleasure for me to give and her to receive the pink, yellow and purple flowers each year on February 7th as we both celebrate my special day. Perhaps I was born in the month of February for a reason. Winter seems so long by this time each year, and when we have had enough of the snow, ice and cold weather, I celebrate my birthday and my mom does too – with flowers that make us think of spring.

Another ritual in my life a few days before my birthday is clipping and gathering a few branches of pussy willow and yellow forsythia, thanking them for giving me the anticipation of spring and the joy of brightening my winter days. I put the branches in a vase of luke-warm water and gaze at their barren branches, trusting in the miracle within them, as they will be blooming in a few days for my birthday — a gift. Both the pussy willow and the forsythia bushes have become large and a little "unruly," some might say, but I cannot bring myself to trim them back any more than clipping only a few spindly branches. The blooms bring spring into my life early. This is called "forcing" – helping the branches to bloom before their natural time outside. The pussy willow will have catkins for flowers – fuzzy to the touch, and the forsythia will have sunshiny yellow blooms. I will dry some of the willow branches for use in arrangements before the catkins are completely in full bloom. Branches of the pussy willow will root in water and can be planted to make new bushes. I have shared many of these rooted branches with friends and family – another friendly *pass-along* plant.

Winter is in my head, but spring is in my heart. -Victor Hugo

The third ritual is writing. I write a birthday page each year. I describe my year, how I feel on this birthday, about this birthday and whatever else I feel like writing. I add it to a notebook with a collection of birthday writings. These pages have become the story of my life through the years. Birthdays are an excellent time to write about the joys and sorrows of the year – recording feelings and what I have learned in the year from the last birthday to this one.

As the years come and go, I celebrate by finding joy and peace within and spending quiet time with close family and friends. I am blessed indeed.

No longer forward nor behind, I look in hope and fear;
But grateful to take the good I find,
the best of now and here.
-John G. Whittier

GRANDMA'S QUILTS

OH, THE STORIES THEY COULD TELL

Quilts, old and new, are a lot like people. The newly made quilts have the best fabrics, good stitching and not a wrinkle – somewhat like young people. Old quilts, the antique, time-worn quilts of years gone by are a little like the *over a certain age* group – a little worn out, having comforted many along the way, used and sometimes abused, with fabrics wrinkled and threadbare in places. Some were used to comfort a sick child or for added warmth in a bedroom on a cold night, and eventually tattered and torn, and after years of use they were thrown away or delegated to the dog's bed.

Old handmade quilts were made to be used, but in time, as fabrics became more abundant, the quilts became masterpieces – they were the Sunday quilts to be put on a bed when company came to visit. Instead of a *nine-patch* or *scrap quilt*, the names and patterns became more sophisticated and varied, like *Tumbling Blocks, Log Cabin, Windmill,* and *Double Wedding Ring,* to name a few. There were many names and patterns to choose from, and the fabric and quilt stores became mainstream as the needlecraft grew in popularity.

I have always admired the beautiful quilts, but most of all the quilts of yesteryear. Perhaps because they were not as sophisticated as today's quilts, but still beautiful. Old quilts hold the stories of the people who made and used them. When I see an old quilt, I want to know the name of the quilt pattern, as well as its history and who made it.

My grandmother was a quilter, making many quilts that she gave away to family. My mom quilted for her church. Alas, I am not a quilter. I am a needlewoman making wool appliqué – not quilts.

My maternal grandmother made quilts of many colors and patterned cotton fabrics in the 50's and 60's. For my high school graduation, Grandma offered me the choice of a quilt or comforter. A comforter was made of heavier fabric with a flannel backing, usually tied instead of quilted. I chose the comforter, even though it was a hard decision, but I was fond of the darker fabrics used in comforters, instead of the pastels Grandma used for her quilts. She asked me what my favorite color was and I said *red*. I remember her saying it could not be all red, and that I needed to choose another color or two to go with the red, so I chose blue. The quilt top was to be navy blue and red, and I told her I liked stars. I was surprised and delighted when presented with the star comforter – it was everything I wanted in a design, and made by Grandma too.

A little over ten years later, Grandma gave me a ribbon quilt she made (this was the second ribbon quilt she made with the many ribbons she won). Grandma's hobbies were growing beautiful flowers in her garden and her quilting. She entered her garden flowers – roses and iris being her favorites – in the flower shows and the county fair and won many ribbons throughout the years. Soon a box was overflowing with ribbons Grandma won and saved, and she decided to make quilt tops from the purple, blue, red and white ribbons. In 1976, Grandma decided to make a second ribbon quilt designed as a bicentennial quilt with a flag in the center (Bicentennial 1776-1976). I asked her if someday I could have this quilt, and she said, "Yes." A few years later she gifted the quilt to me. I love the patriotic motif, the ribbons she won, and knowing that Grandma put it all together in her own design. It had to be hard to work with the material, as the ribbons were satiny and slippery. My hope is that this quilt will always stay in the family or perhaps in a quilt history museum, such as the internationally-renowned quilt museum in Lincoln, Nebraska.

Seeing Grandma's love of quilting and with my growing interest in the history of antique quilts, I took a class on dating antique quilts by Barbara Brackman. I learned about the fabrics and patterns of old quilts, and my interest grew further when I opened up an antiques mall with many vendors. I saw many quilts come and go at the antiques mall and used my newly-gained knowledge of dating old quilts, which increased my love for the quilts even more. My collection continued to grow. I collected patriotic quilts, others were made with strictly the heart motif, some were friendship quilts with names embroidered on them, and some were crazy quilts – and many others. My favorite has always been the *Log Cabin* design, of which there are many variations. I specifically preferred the ones with the red square in the middle of each of the blocks, representing a *light in the window* or *fire in the hearth*.

Along the way, a quilt would cross my path that I wanted to know more about, and I would start researching again. One such case was a red and white quilt with over a hundred names embroidered on it in a wheel design. The many names were embroidered as the spokes on the wheel circles. I would venture to say that 98% of the quilts from long ago were not dated, nor were they marked with the name of the maker. But this red and white quilt was marked with many names as well as a date, city, and the name of a church. In looking further, I realized this was a friendship quilt made by members of this church, probably as a going away gift for a minister. I called the local church whose name was embroidered on the quilt, and the person who answered the phone said she would have someone get back to me. Within the hour, three women came through the front door of my antiques mall and asked to see the quilt. They told me they were working on a 100-year reunion celebration for the church, and this quilt would be a wonderful addition hanging in a place of honor. The three ladies had known nothing about the quilt before my phone call – this quilt had been lost and now found. We were all in tears knowing this quilt was going back home. Oh, the story this quilt could tell of its travels to get to its final destination, which was the place it originally started from.

Up until this time I had only read about, but had never seen, a quilt with a *humble block* in the design. One evening, one of my vendors brought in a beautiful quilt made with dark colors and a red square in the middle of each block – a *Log Cabin* quilt. There was no cotton fabric in this quilt. It was made of rayon gabardine and wool and was visually striking. I knew immediately that this quilt would be added to my growing collection. It is a large quilt and has been one of my favorites over the years. This showy quilt was made by the Amish or Mennonite people. All fabric used is dark and plain, except for the red squares. There is no design or pattern in the material – except at the bottom corner there is a block made of patterned fabric, which is called the *humble block,* to symbolize their belief that humans are not perfect; only God is perfect. The one block is completely different from all the others, and this was done on purpose. I have never seen another quilt again with the *humble block* in it. I am humbled when I see this quilt. Oh, the story this quilt could tell.

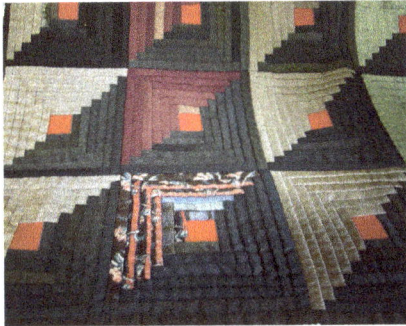

The history of old quilts is fascinating, and I have been greatly interested in reading of the quilts hung as signs during the time of the Underground Railroad. Some have disputed this history, but others have written books noting the oral history of this happening. I appreciate that quilts played a part in many slaves' safe escape and journey to the north – some quilts denoted a safe place, and some told of danger. Oh, the stories these quilts could tell.

A memorable find for me was a message from my departed grandmother. I believe in listening to my instincts, intuition and the ancestors whispering in my ear. Grandma has been gone from us for a long time now. And so, the story goes like this:

My sister and I were planning to meet at her workplace, but when I arrived she informed me she could not leave for 45 minutes, so I said I would just wait or I would be back later. I knew of an antique shop about a block away, and I knew the shop owners, but it had been a long time since I had been in their shop. This was the perfect opportunity to stop in and say hello. As I turned around to go to the shop, I kept telling myself I didn't need to buy another thing and I should wait in the car reading my book until my sister was through with her job. But the shop was so close by and it was calling to me.

I walked into the store and visited awhile with the owners in the front room before walking through the shop, looking at the wonderful things they had collected and were for sale. I didn't get very far, as something was catching my interest out of the corner of my eye in the room to my left. I was being pulled in that direction. I walked over to it and stopped. The quilt-like wall hanging in front of me hung high up on a tall wall. It resembled a *Log Cabin* design. The colors were dark – the kind of coloring I liked. It was small, a bit over a yardstick in width and about five foot in height. The seven-inch blocks were faded; some were black and others olive green. All the blocks were edged with feather stitching, and there were four 1-½ inch red squares in each block. I was entranced by this wall hanging. It could not be called a quilt by any means (it was not quilted nor tied) nor called a *Log Cabin* design by any stretch of the imagination except for the four red squares (lights) in the middle, which were a unique part of the design. The four-inch strip around the four sides had been a navy color at one time but had faded to a denim/gray blue. As I got closer I saw there were names embroidered on the blocks. I started to see names that were familiar to an area my mom was from early in her life, and then closer to the middle of the wall hanging I saw my grandmother's name – *Lydia Meeske*. My knees got weak and I gasped, telling the antiques dealer standing next to me that this was my maternal grandmother's name stitched in this piece. I then asked her for history – *where did she find it?* She said she bought it at an auction in a nearby town, and she had taken it to a recent flea market, which I knew my mother and two of my sisters had attended a couple weeks earlier (this flea market draws many thousands of people each year). I knew now why my sister was running late and why I was in this antiques shop on this day, at this moment in time, and why my mom and sisters did not notice it at the flea market. I believe Grandma wanted me to have it. She knew of my love for history and old quilts and knew I would care for and appreciate it. And I do. My research found that it was a friendship quilt made in the 1930's. The 40 blocks were embroidered and made by the *Willing Workers Club* in or near Daykin, Nebraska. My grandmother was a member of this group and embroidered her name on one of the blocks. It was given to someone in the group who perhaps was moving away. Along the way it was lost, likely sold at auction with other blankets.

This wall hanging has hung on my bedroom wall ever since the day Grandma led me to it. Oh, the stories this quilt could tell from the time Grandma stitched her name lovingly into a piece of cloth to being found and in the hands of a granddaughter who was perhaps meant to find it and have it after all, more than 75 years later.

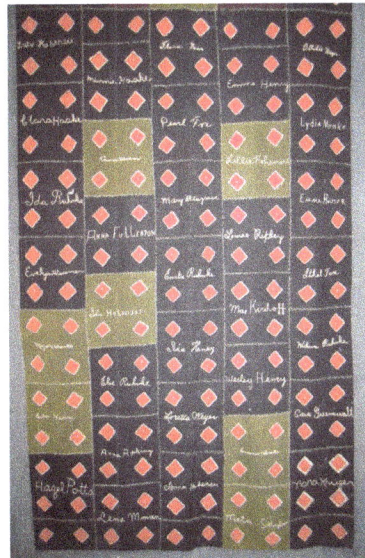

SINCE THE TIME WOMEN BEGAN DOING NEEDLEWORK and making quilts, a part of their lives have been stitched into the fibers of these quilts. The stitches, the feel of the cotton fabric, the pattern – all were made with loving hands. Quilting was done in happy times and sad times. As the stitches were being made in the quilt, the happy times were stitching and visiting with other women and talking about raising their children, or working through anxiety and depression, perhaps pricking their finger with the sharp needle and a drop of blood would stain the quilt forever. Or another time stitching through tears falling on the quilt after the loss of a dear loved one. Old quilts, including my grandma's, have many stories to tell.

March

THE VIEW FROM MY WINDOW

*The first day of spring is one thing
and the first spring day is another.
The difference between them
is sometimes as great as a month.*
-Van Dyke

Spring arrives – or so the calendar says in the month of March! Many times March arrives like the proverbial lamb and other times like the ferocious lion, and every March is different. March is long awaited, as it is the month of the Spring Equinox, celebrated on the first day of spring in the third week of the month. This is the time when day and night are equal and we celebrate the rebirth of the land.

March is a month of transition when Mother Nature cannot quite figure out if it is winter or spring – one day it is 20 degrees and a few days later it is close to 70 degrees. Winter still hangs on in the Midwest – barely.

It was a long, tiresome and sometimes brutal winter, but the snow has now melted enough for me to check on the snowdrops, crocus, tulips and daffodils popping their heads up. Mother Nature is quietly shedding her heavy winter coat. I want to hurry to finish the inside jobs on my list so when the warm temperatures lure me outside my door, I will feel like staying awhile, cleaning up the dried grasses, looking for the new plants growing and seeing what survived the bitter winter weather that is now *hopefully* behind us. There is a lingering chill in the air in March, but the sunshine and spring fever has held me firmly in its grip these past few days. I know I cannot trust the fickle March weather – one day nice and the next day bitter cold again. I cannot put away my winter coat yet, but the thought is there, and soon it will happen.

The grass is greening and the wild onions are appearing. The birds will be nesting and the Canadian geese are honking their way back to the lake announcing, *We are here!* Hopefully the same pair of geese will return to build their nest of cattail reeds and hatch their babies as they did last year on the edge of the watershed lake.

The pussy willow branches I clipped and put in a vase of water in February have large fuzzy catkins now and some have rooted, so I will put the rooted ones in a flower pot filled with soil to plant in another spot later on or give to a friend — they help usher in spring.

The plants and trees and flowers are taking notice of the warmer days. The buds are forming, and later in the month the daffodils and forsythia will burst into bright color. Yellow seems to be the color most favored by Mother Nature the end of March into April. I love the little sunshine yellow crocus peeking out of the earth, along with the purple ones, a sure sign of spring. Last fall I bemoaned the aches and pains of an aging body while planting a lot of bulbs and will be rewarded this spring with many more blooms.

> *First a howling blizzard woke up*
> *Then the rain came down to soak us.*
> *And now before the eye can focus – Crocus!*
> – Lilja Rogers

Several years back I took my mom with me to the garden center and she commented that for a gardener it was like a kid going into a candy store. We loved seeing the flowers and bought more than we needed, as they were hard to resist. And now my mom cannot get out and about, so I send her garden magazines to look at, because once a gardener always a gardener, even when the body won't cooperate.

Winter hangs on too long for the gardener who likes to dig in the warmed earth and is eager to plant the first seed. Spring is waiting in the wings to make its entrance, and soon it will play its part in Nature like a drama waiting to unfold. Spring cannot come soon enough for me.

Some years our spring comes early with the warming temperatures and some years it is late, staying cool into the month of April. Now with global warming everything is changing. This time of year, I am most impatient and excited to see the first bulbs peeking out of the earth as if looking around to be sure all is safe for them to continue to grow upwards. I am giddy with delight at each plant I see budded or flowering, and I can never get enough of the flowers that herald spring. By the end of March, the little irises from my great grandmother are blooming, and I hear her voice whispering in the winds around me.

When the winds of March
are wakening the crocuses and crickets,
Did you ever find a fairy
near budding little thickets?
And when she sees you
creeping up to get a closer look
She tumbles through the daffodils
playing hide and seek.
-Marjorie Burrows

The first greening in the woods is the poison ivy, followed by the long canes of wild rose bushes and wild honeysuckle. Before the leaves appear on the trees, I can see through the woods and under-story growth into clearings beyond, but soon it will be all briars and tangles and hard to walk through or see through. It then becomes a safe haven for the birds and wildlife. In my times of solitude at the end of March, I listen for the Peepers, the sound of spring arriving.

I pause to think how hard it must have been for the Native Americans and the early settlers to survive the long hard winters. I believe they were impatient for spring to arrive with the first green leaves of dandelion and the wild onions to eat. I am thankful spring has come once again to my little corner of the world.

Pipit Daffodil

THE MARCH FULL MOON

*In the month of March, the full moon is called many names, including *Mud Moon, Sap Moon, Worm Moon, Full Crow Moon,* and *Full Crust Moon* and was considered the last full moon of Winter.

I know why it is called the *Mud Moon* — oh my, we DO have mud here in the country as the ground is thawing, but soon the spring breezes will dry it out. The *Sap Moon,* in the month of March, was the traditional time the early settlers tapped the maple trees to gather the sap to make maple syrup.

The March full moon was also called the *Worm Moon* as the frozen ground began to thaw with temperatures warming and the earthworms appeared, to the delight of hungry robins waiting for this food on the surface of the ground.

March full moon was a time anticipated by humans, animals and birds alike. The earth in March is awakening.

IN THE GARDEN IN MARCH

Every gardener knows that under the cloak of winter
lies a miracle....
A bulb opening to the light,
A bud straining to unfurl,
And the anticipation nurtures our dream.
- Barbara Winkler

SNOWDROPS

Snowdrops are the little harbingers of spring and a joy to watch bloom. I anticipate their arrival, blooming through the snow here in my neck of the woods. I cannot have too many of these dainty sweet little teardrop flowers, the color of newly fallen snow, and I impatiently wait to see the first one each March.

The little bulbs of this plant multiply, so I share with others as a *pass-along* plant, or move some to another section of the garden. I ask myself, *Can one really have too many of them?* I used to plant them in with the herbs and flowers, but the following March I could not see them bloom because the dried herbs were covering them. Now I plant them in an open spot or around a tree, where they bloom

peacefully in the sunshine as the tree has not leafed out yet. This is what gardening is all about – finding what works best for our plants. When my plants are happy, I am happy. Gardening keeps teaching us lessons, and hopefully we pay attention.

TIP: *To prevent fungus from forming on little seedlings started indoors, I use a weak chamomile tea instead of plain water to moisten the little seedlings. Using a dropper on the tiniest seedlings also is a good idea. I use dried chamomile to make a cup of medium strong hot tea. I let it cool down and then dilute to make a quart of water for the seedlings. It works well.*

My to-do list before the first day of spring:

- Find the frozen elderberries still in the freezer and make syrup or jelly before the next crop is ready to pick and freeze.
- Make more lavender soap to carry me through the next busy six months.
- Gather together the bottles to make herb vinegars.
- Make tick and mosquito repellent to use when I am outside this summer. I don't like spraying chemicals on my body, so I make my own.
- Celebrate the first day of spring!

Spirit of Spring, thy coverlet of snow hath fallen from thee,
with its fringe of frost,
And where the river late did overflow
Sway fragile white anemones, wind-tost,
And in the woods stand snowdrops, half asleep,
With drooping heads — sweet dreamers so long lost.
- from *The Waking of Spring* by Olive Custance (b. 1874)

IN THE KITCHEN IN MARCH

While the days are still cool I enjoy making corn chowder. This recipe makes a big pot full, so it is good to serve when I invite guests over or I can share a pint or a quart with a friend.

CORN CHOWDER
1 yellow onion, diced
1 clove garlic, diced and crushed
3 celery stalks, diced small
Coconut oil or bacon grease
2 c. chicken broth
2 c. milk
3 T. butter
1/4 c. flour
3 c. diced raw potatoes
1/4 c. diced fresh red pepper
16 oz. pkg. frozen corn
Salt and pepper to taste
2 c. chopped ham, in small pieces

1 T. dried parsley
1 T. All-Purpose Herb Blend or to taste (January recipe)
Crumbled cooked bacon and shredded cheddar cheese

Sauté the onion, garlic and celery in oil or grease covering pan with lid. When translucent in color, add the broth, potatoes and red pepper, and cook 10-15 minutes or until potatoes are almost done. While cooking, make a roux in a separate pan: melt 3 T. butter and add 1/4 c. flour. Mix well and whisk in 2 c. milk. Heat while stirring until thickened. Add roux, corn, salt and pepper, ham, parsley and herb mix. Add more water/broth as needed for desired consistency.

Immediately before serving, add 1 Tbsp. finely shredded cheddar cheese and/or crumbed cooked bacon to top of soup as garnish, if desired. Adjust seasonings to taste.

THE SONG OF SPRING

What would happen if we lived in a way
that listened to the voices in the land –
Of the pine, and the oak, the ancestors singing as we walked
down the valley where they too, once walked?
–Ann Ambrecht, *Thin Places*

I hear the Peepers!

It is March, and I hear the unmistakable sound of a chorus of frogs singing in high-pitched voices all at once. It is the arrival of the Spring Peepers! I wait with anticipation for this sound each year, and when I hear it I know spring has truly and finally arrived. I sit on the front porch listening to the *Song of Spring*, the sound of nature coming alive all around me again. There is no turning back now – the peepers are here! Living in the Midwest it is a common and most welcoming sound of spring, and I look forward to hearing the peeper's song continue in the weeks ahead.

The sound of the peepers can be almost deafening, but I never tire of it. And when I finally hear it breaking the quiet without any forewarning, I stop and thank Mother Earth for these little peepers singing their hearts out, making me mindful of life around me, and all the while they are looking for a mate.

The little peepers, as we fondly call them in the Midwest, are chorus frogs. The males are the only ones that sing, and in the early spring they start singing for a mate non-stop. These little frogs have been in a deep winter sleep in the mud of a pond or creek nearby. The peepers need to live near water so the female can lay eggs in the water, and they are found in farm ponds, wetlands and woods. If I have seen a peeper, I have not recognized it as a peeper, only a small frog, and I have looked for them. Like an old friend, I am always sure I will recognize one when I see it.

Peepers are said to be brown and only about one and a half inches long. They are nocturnal and mainly active at night, but I hear them singing during the days also in March. It does seem that once they start to sing they really do not want to stop. Hearing the peepers has become a spring ritual – like Mother Nature sounding her trumpet, to let us know spring has now arrived.

Like many other species, the little peepers have been put on an endangered list in the Midwest because of wetland areas being destroyed for developments. If you have peepers in your area, celebrate them and educate the children about them, as the next generation may be the only hope for these little peepers to survive.

When I hear the little peepers may be in trouble of becoming extinct, Rachel Carson's book, *Silent Spring*, takes on even more meaning once again for me. It would not be spring without the sounds of springtime – birds chirping, bees buzzing and the little peepers singing.

GREAT-GRANDMA'S MINI IRIS

$\mathcal{B}$ig things come in small packages.

The little irises that bloom in my garden each spring may be small, but they are big on attraction. I love the sweet little purple iris that bloom mid-to-late March each and every year. What a delight to see the first bud ready to open! I watch each morning for buds to appear and then to finally burst into bloom. Each evening I cover the iris patch so the deer won't find them and the little iris can fulfill their destiny – to bloom in my garden.

The start of my little iris patch was given to me by my mom, and the story goes that they were originally grown by my great-grand-mother Amelia. They were passed on to my great Aunt Dora and my grandmother Lydia and on to my mom, Verneeda, and now me. The time has come for me to pass along the little iris to my daugh-ter's flower garden and tell her the story.

The little iris seem to grow and begin blooming overnight, and a patch of purple appears on the earth. They are a connection to my past and give me hope for today. I know the trees are listening and hear me talk to Great-Grandma, who died when I was seventeen. I feel her smiling as she hears me and sees the little iris blooming in my garden and my enjoyment of it all.

The patch of a dozen or more dark blooms catches everyone's eye as they walk by and exclaim, *"What is this little flower?"* I don't know for sure if it is actually a miniature iris or a dwarf iris or something in between. Someone once told me they were called *flags*. It does not really matter what others call them – I call them *Great-Grandma's little iris*. I have several clumps, making sure I will always have them in my life in the spring. The blooming little iris patches are part of the whole picture of springtime and my life.

Every spring, I delight in picking one to bring inside and put it in a small bottle and think how my mom, my grandma, and my great-grandmother would have done the same each spring, and my heart warms.

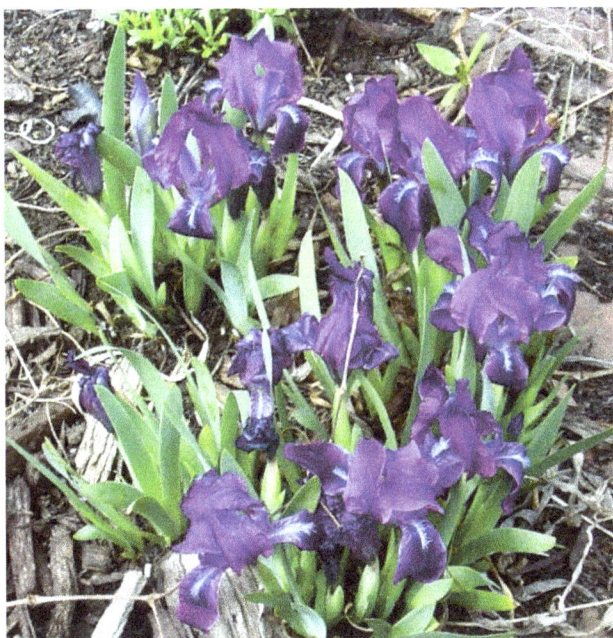

Mini iris passed down through generations from great-grandmother Amelia

HOME NESTING AND BIRD NESTS

I suppose I am a sparrow, a stay-at-home bird.
- Gladys Taber

The females of every species "nest," whether we are human, animal or bird.

Moving from state to state and house to house, I have found the job of *nesting* to be enjoyable. The many boxes to unpack, shelves to fill, and putting every item in the right spot for use and display is often daunting at first, but it is all a part of the process of our settling in – in other words, *nesting*. Once we are nested into a new abode we feel peaceful, happy, and ready to put down roots – all part of nesting and making a house a home.

Each time I move, I designate an old open cupboard for a display of bird nests. These nests are carefully packed and unpacked, move after move, and have taken many years to collect. *(And I must say this now – it is illegal to take a songbird nest in the wild that might be used by a nesting bird).*

My friends know I collect nests, so they watch for a situation that might garner a bird's nest, like the cutting down of a tree or shrub where a nest resides. I have found that a nest blown out of a tree during a storm cannot be put back into another place in a tree and stay there. The nest is hard to re-anchor in place as birds would have done it, so I collect it. Sometimes trees and shrubs are cut out of the roadside ditches by county employees, and the nests are doomed for destruction.

One beautiful autumn day, while living in Nebraska, I heard a lot of commotion along the country road where I lived. I was very concerned, so I walked to the end of my lane where I could plainly see what was going on. I saw wonderful trees and shrubs being cut down in the road "right of way." I walked up the road to look more closely and found eight state workers (only four doing the work and the others watching while my tax dollars were paying for this!) and I was livid. I love my country roads with their wild vegetation, and the workers were cutting down small to medium sized trees and many wild plum thickets, completely clearing out and destroying the country road ditch of any vegetation whatsoever. This was a one-mile stretch of road, dead-ending on both ends, barely traveled except for three people living on the road. In my humble opinion, the shrubs and small trees were hurting no one – in fact, they were helping prevent soil erosion, providing protection for birds and wildlife, and were away from overhead wires.

Gone were the small young trees and saplings, and gone were the wild plum bushes that bloomed so fragrantly each spring for the bees and produced wonderful fruit in the late summer for the birds to eat and for me to make jelly.

There would no longer be places for birds to nest or pheasant and quail to hide, or rabbits and raccoons and other wildlife to live along my country road. I asked the workers many questions about why, and did they have to do this, and why could it not be left alone, but with the "powers that be" I knew it was a lost cause. I obtained a phone number and called "the boss," questioning him for the next half hour as workers continued to cut down everything in the ditch. I also wrote a letter to the editor of the local newspaper.

The next morning, I surveyed the roadside destruction and shed tears. I discovered bird nests laying down, still attached to the wild plum branches. The shredder would be shredding every last stick in the ditch within the week, so I gathered the nests – remnants of man's disrespect for nature and the birds' ingenuity in constructing a perfect little home.

This was how my collection of nests began, and my collection now consists of the finch nests I saved that day, as well as a couple robin nests, a cardinal nest and an oriole nest. The robin nests blew out of big trees during storms, and the cardinal nest was in a big old vine running along a fence that was being pruned out, and we didn't find it until it was too late. The oriole nest is my pride and joy, as my son lovingly brought it back for me from a hunting trip when he found it hanging from a broken limb — and what a work of art this nest is! I struggle to understand how a small bird with just a beak could make a nest for its eggs hanging out on the end of a branch. It is a perfectly elongated nest with the remnants of an old discarded cassette tape woven through it, making it look a bit comical and very resourceful.

I am hoping to one day add a tiny hummingbird nest to my collection but will not take one – it will have to happen when a branch with a nest falls or is found on the ground. Hummingbirds are here for only a short time in our part of the country.

My collection of nests sits in an old black painted antique cupboard with a small electric candlestick light illuminating the nests, giving them a place of importance and respect. One nest sits in a small shallow old wooden bowl, another on a small wooden plate, and another is still attached to a part of the branch. I have a painted canvas of a bird nest that sits at the back of the shelf, and I have discovered there are books on the subject of bird's nests, so I read and collect them too.

I encourage everyone to admire and respect a bird nest in a tree, especially it if is occupied. If you find a bird nest that has fallen out of a tree, consider starting a collection of your own while you are nesting in your home.

Tip: *Before bringing inside, "de-bug" by putting the nest into a zipper plastic bag, spraying with bug spray and sitting it in the sun a few days.*

> *The greatest achievement was at first, for a time, a dream.*
> *The oak sleeps in the acorn,*
> *the bird waits in the egg,*
> *and in the highest vision of the soul, a waking angel stirs.*
> *Dreams are the seedlings of realities.*
> –James Allen

SOLITUDE

Solitude: an undervalued precious resource.
-unknown

*T*oday I sit alone. There have been many times in my life when I have been lonely. And now I find there are times I am alone but find peace in solitude. I think of loneliness and solitude as close cousins to one other. In each, I find my other self and in each, I found the need to recognize whether this is a positive or negative place to be. Life circumstances and time teach us the difference – and the choice then becomes ours to make.

After my husband died suddenly, I spent a few years of grieving before moving to another state to be near my daughter and her family. I left behind other family, many friends, our home we had built together, and familiar places. I told myself this was another adjustment on this path called *Life*. Each big change or adjustment in life requires soul-searching, and the end result can be far different than what we thought it would be.

I mistakenly thought of loneliness and solitude as one and the same, but in time I came to understand the difference. One is chosen and the other imposed – by self or by others. Loneliness was moving away from familiar people and places to where everything was different and I knew no one except my daughter and her family. Having close friends to talk things over with is critical at any age, but especially in the last third of life, where I now find myself. The challenge of making friends becomes increasingly more difficult as we age. Being around people is one thing, but actually making a connection can be challenging. I had no history with people I met in this new place I moved to and now call home. I found it hard to become a part of an established group that had been together for many years. Being an outsider was something I had not anticipated. Being lonely is isolating. Trips to the grocery store became more to talk to someone than to get food. I secluded myself in my own four walls, and it became more negative with each passing day. After trying to find friends (something that has always been easy for me to do), long stretches of loneliness and not connecting deeply with others, I found something else happening – my time with myself shifted from loneliness to solitude.

Solitude is a good place to be these days. It can get lonely, but because I recognize it as my choice now, I can find peace while reading a book, being creative, and spending time in nature connecting with Mother Earth. Time alone allows me to gain perspective in what is ahead in my life, taking time to reflect and find more joy. Solitude has taught me mindfulness and living with intention, and it became a spiritual quest.

Although I have now made good friends in this new place, I find I am my own best company and my own best friend. I savor and protect my times of Solitude. Solitude is Peace.

April

THE VIEW FROM MY WINDOW

Oh, how fresh the wind is blowing,
April! April! Are you here?
See! The sky is bright and clear,
Oh, how green the grass is growing!
April! April! Are you here?
-Dora R. Goodale, 1866-1953

*B*lessed Spring! So much beauty to behold!

The world outside my window appeared eerie and mysterious on this foggy April morning. As I walked in my garden I noticed how still and quiet it was with no breeze. I listened for the birds and did not hear them in the silence of the fog – it takes sunshine for me to fully awaken too. This was a morning when I didn't want to disturb a thing. I only wanted to sip my cup of hot herbal tea and savor my surroundings. And later, as I headed back into the warmth of my house, I took a deep breath – I did not want to let go of this moment in time. I loved the musty smell of the earth around me on this April morning, with the silence, the fog and the mystery of it all. Our world is made up of senses – seeing, touching, smelling, hearing, and I found it all in my foggy garden.

This is spring in my little corner of the world – foggy one morning, rainy the next, and sunshine streaming brightly in the window the following day. I savor all of these mornings when spring wants to firmly take hold.

As the meadows and woods are greening rapidly, I have been foraging and picking the new green leaves of the wild nutritious weeds. My sluggish winter body is trying to adapt to the busy time of spring, knowing there will be much work needing to be done. I make a cup of hot tea from the herbs to detoxify my system and help my body adapt to the busier lifestyle to come. More fresh greens are definitely on the menu these days. I add freshly cut nettle tops to my quiché or in a pan of scrambled eggs. Chickweed and young dandelion leaves are added to my salad and perhaps a young violet or plantain leaf. I pick extra dandelion leaves, drying them on a clean white dishtowel on my kitchen island. I will dry a lot of greens to crumble into soup in the winter and add to tea. Our ancestral mothers must have been overjoyed to see the first greens appear in the spring after a long and harsh winter when food was sparse.

THE EARTH IS WARMING FROM THE SUN'S RAYS, THE days are becoming longer, the birds are singing their song, and I long to be in the fresh air. Early April I am poking and prodding the earth in this season of rebirth to plant my herbs and vegetables and flowers in my gardens. I will also take note of what did and did not survive the cold harsh winter months now past.

RAIN SETTLES ON THE PARCHED AND AWAKENING EARTH and soaks in like a sponge on this early April day. I am reminded of the proverbial saying, *"April showers bring May flowers."* The Midwest is still too dry, and I know this time of year can bring the spring storms with spectacular lightning showcasing the dark skies. The lightning is followed by the booming sounds of drums in the skies, creating a showcase of light and sound in the heavens above.

Cloud formations are strangely beautiful, and I hurry to take a picture of this ever-changing stormy sky today. The skies can be quite threatening when thunderstorms are predicted, so I watch closely. The springtime worry is that the thunderstorms can develop into full blown tornadoes here in the Midwest, so I am always prepared to run for cover if need be. But the violent thunderstorms pass on by with only rain on this April day. The spring rain was needed and washes everything clean while giving parched Mother Earth a long cool drink. And after the rains, a stunning rainbow appears, and now and then I am blessed to see a double rainbow over the trees in the woods close to my home and beyond.

As the earth recovers from the storm, I look into the woods and the tree leaves are more vibrantly green than ever. I am amazed at the many shades of green in Nature's paint box. I love color, and the many shades and layers it creates in the landscape around my country home fill my senses.

GREEN IS EVERYWHERE THIS MONTH, BUT I THINK *YELLOW* is Nature's pick for a favorite spring fashion color. In April, the dandelions start to bloom yellow, the daffodils are in bloom now and the forsythia – which was blooming on April fool's day this year – waves its long yellow flowering branches in the breeze trying to get my attention — as if she needs to. The sparkly yellow of spring cannot be missed, perhaps because it looks so joyfully bright with the greens surrounding in the woods and meadow. And then, there is the serendipity of a red male cardinal flitting in the yellow flowering forsythia branches, perhaps showing off a little to get the attention of its mate or looking for a place to build a nest this spring – it is all sensory overload! I adore this time of year, whether it is a 40-degree cooler day or a warm 70-degree perfect day, a rainy day or a day full of sunshine – it all says spring to me.

Forsythia is pure joy:
There is not an ounce, not a glimmer of sadness in forsythia.
Pure, undiluted untouched joy.
-Anne Morrow Lindbergh

Flowers seem to be more beautiful each spring, or perhaps it is that we have forgotten over the long winter how beautiful spring really is. The usual perennials are eagerly anticipated and do not disappoint. I love the various colors of the patches of tulips, the little grape hyacinths, crocus, daffodils and all that blooms in my garden.

I love spring anywhere,
but if I could choose I would always greet it in a garden.
-Ruth Stout

By mid-April, the trees are blooming and leafing out and the lilacs are blooming too. It is almost too much to take in after the dull gray, brown and white of winter.

MY FEATHERED FRIENDS ARE NOT AT THE FEEDERS AS much now, as they are busy with mating season, preparing their nesting spots, while some are actually nesting in early April. The jenny wren has not put in her appearance yet and won't until the end of the month or even next month. Ms. Wren usually nests fairly close to the house, so I have been hanging a few things around the back porch, like an old gourd and a basket, but if she doesn't appear soon house finches will claim those locations for their nests.

APRIL BRINGS TWO CELEBRATIONS THAT ARE CLOSE TO my heart – Earth Day and Arbor Day. Taking care of the earth, where we live, and planting a tree for myself and generations to come is a spiritual practice for me, good for the body as well as the soul.

Sunrise with peach blossoms

THE APRIL FULL MOON

We no longer live our lives from full moon to full moon, nor do we name the moons to recognize and remind us what month or season it is. Today I find the names interesting and wonder what other names the moons were called. As times change, would we name the moons differently? Most of the time, or all of the time, I believe we do not think much about the full moon or what it means. We look at a calendar or computer to remind us of the time of year it is. I watch the moon from night to night as it gets fuller, waiting for the full moon in all of its glory to appear.

April gives us a *Pink Full Moon*, named for the wild ground phlox, which is one of the earliest wildflowers of the spring. I look over a lavender-pink field of henbit blooming now on an April day and wonder if this little plant was also used in naming the April *Pink Full Moon*.

The April full moon is also known as *Frog Full Moon* when the little amphibian creatures make themselves known in the wetlands and the marshes near the ponds. The chorus frogs, or spring peepers as I call them, make a happy sound by the end of March and the entire month of April.

Other recognized names for the April full moon are *Full Sprouting Grass Moon*, *Egg Full Moon,* and with the tribes that lived closer to the sea, it was the *Shad Full Moon,* as this was the time the shad swam upstream to spawn.

We are all looking at the same moon.

IN THE GARDEN IN APRIL

All through the long winter,
I dream of my garden.
On the first day of spring I dig my fingers
deep into the soft earth.
I can feel its energy and my spirit soars.
-Helen Hayes

I started my early lettuce patch a little differently this year. In the past, I have shared a lot of my garden with rabbits and deer, so this year I started the lettuce seeds in a big old gray granite dishpan with a few rusty holes in the bottom. I am able to sit it up higher than the inquisitive noses and mouths of rabbits, and it also gives me the opportunity to bring it inside on a cold night if I choose or if I feel the deer might come to visit. It is a delight to see the little seeds sprout, connecting me once more to the miracle of a seed growing into a plant for food.

As I walk through the garden patch and see new plants emerging, I know the fairies have been up to their mischief and fun in my garden once again. I notice plants where I did not plant them, and I thank the fairies for their help and leave them to grow, creating the wild landscape around me. And I watch for the dainty wild violets eagerly in the spring, as I know the fairies love to live in wild violet patches.

More than anything I must have flowers always, always.
-Claude Monet

There are many baby plants growing here and there from self-seeding, and they will grow to become gifts to give to someone else. I call these *pass-along* plants, which I gently repot to give to a friend, adding a little note listing the plant's virtues. One of the little plants I share is the tiny miniature purple iris that were passed down in our family and came originally from my great-grandmother's garden. A lot of my flower garden is made up of *pass-along* plants that have been given to me by others.

Don't wait for someone to bring you flowers.
Plant your own garden
and decorate your own soul.
-Luther Burbank

The wild plum thickets along the banks of the running creek nearby are now in full bloom. I open the windows on a nice day, and the wind gently wafts the fragrance into my kitchen, and then I can no longer resist. I walk to the thicket to clip a few short branches to put in a vase on my country farm table. I am careful to take only a few branches to enjoy, knowing there will be wild plums later in the summer, providing food for the birds and jelly for me. I stop and take my shoes off so my bare feet can touch and connect with Mother Earth on this fine April day.

To everything there is a season.

IN THE KITCHEN IN APRIL

In the spring, rhubarb becomes a prized plant in my
garden and then in my kitchen.

I protect and nurture this plant all the while thinking of its deliciousness once cooked or baked.

FAVORITE SPRING RHUBARB DESSERT

This yummy recipe is from my Aunt Maxine, and every spring the family looks forward to this – several times.

Bake in a 9x12 Pyrex dish, butter the bottom of pan, and set oven at 350 degrees.
4 c. fresh rhubarb, cut up (I have also used frozen)
1 c. sugar
1 – 3 oz. pkg. strawberry Jell-O (strawberry/banana is good too)
1 box white cake mix
1 stick butter
1 c. water

In a bowl, add the cut-up rhubarb, sugar and Jell-O and mix together. Pour into baking pan. In another bowl put the white cake mix and butter only and crumb together (I use hand mixer). Pour this crumb mixture over the rhubarb mix in pan. Sprinkle one cup water over the crumb mixture using a tablespoon to dribble water over mix. Bake about 40 minutes at 350 degrees. Serve warm with ice cream.

RHUBARB CAKE with Crumble topping

This recipe came from a rug-hooking student of mine (Sandra M.) when I lived in Estes Park, Colorado. It is now a favorite for serving to groups or family. I prefer to use the cut-up frozen rhubarb from my freezer (seems to add more moisture) and can be made any time of year.

1 stick butter
1 c. brown sugar, packed lightly
1 extra large egg or 2 smaller ones
1 tsp. vanilla
1/2 tsp. salt
2 c. flour
1 tsp. soda
2 c. fresh rhubarb, cut into 1/2-inch size pieces (or 2 c. frozen, thawed & partially drained)
1 c. sour milk *(made by using 1 c. room temp. milk & adding 1 ½ T. apple cider vinegar. Let stand to thicken a few minutes before using – don't use pasteurized milk that has gone bad)*.

TOPPING for rhubarb cake
2 tsp. melted butter
1/2 c. brown sugar
1/2 c. chopped pecans or walnuts
1 tsp. cinnamon

Preheat oven to 350 degrees. Method for cake: Cream together butter and brown sugar. Add egg and vanilla. Add dry ingredients alternately with sour milk. Mix well. Fold in rhubarb. Spoon batter into greased 9x12 glass pan.

Topping: Mix until crumbly and sprinkle mixture on top of batter. Bake for 45 minutes or until toothpick comes out clean.

RHUBARB/STRAWBERRY JAM

Appliqué student Deb, from central Nebraska, kindly gifted me with a jar of this jam and it quickly became a family favorite. It is delicious on toasted English muffins, rolls, or toast. The recipe calls for 5 c. rhubarb but I changed it so my grandkids wouldn't suspect the rhubarb was in it – we just call it strawberry jam when they are around. Someday I'll tell them rhubarb is what makes it taste so good.

Only three ingredients: the rhubarb mix, sugar and Jell-O
5 c. chopped rhubarb (or a combination of rhubarb and straw-berries)
4 c. sugar

STIR THE ABOVE TWO INGREDIENTS TOGETHER (sugar/fruit) and let sit overnight in refrigerator covered. Next day put in stainless steel large pan and bring the mix to a boil and simmer for 7-8 minutes. (You will see it start to thicken up but don't want it too thick as it also thickens as it cools down). Remove from heat and stir in:

1 pkg. (3 oz.) strawberry Jell-O (or strawberry/banana)

Ladle into clean jars, put lids on and refrigerate (this is a refrigerator jam).

Note: *I mash the rhubarb with a potato masher as it is cooking to break up the rhubarb more. I have never processed this with the canning method as I just make up a batch as needed and refrigerate. I freeze cut up rhubarb and strawberries in 5 c. packages so it is ready to use to make this jam.*

RHUBARB PIE

This recipe came from high school close friend Judy B.

1 unbaked piecrust in a 9- inch pie pan
4 c. rhubarb chopped in 1/2 in. size pieces
1 ¼ c. sugar
¼ tsp. salt
3 T. flour
2 T. melted butter
1 egg, well beaten

COMBINE SUGAR, SALT, FLOUR, AND BUTTER. MIX together with the rhubarb. Add the beaten egg into the rhubarb mixture. Place in the piecrust.

TOPPING FOR RHUBARB PIE

1/2 c. sugar
1/2 c. flour
Dash salt
1/4 c. butter

Mix the sugar, flour and salt well, cut in butter. Put over top of rhubarb mixture. Bake 45 minutes in 350 degree oven until done.

Note: *This topping can be used for any kind of fruit pie.*

HERBS

How do I love thee – let me count the ways.

Herbs are a big part of my life today, and many herb plants grow in my garden and always will. I grow them for the aromatherapy, culinary uses and for medicinal purposes.

I started growing herbs when I found plants at a garden center and noticed how they smelled. These were aromatic herbs, as many herbs are. Fragrance was my first attraction to these plants. I knew nothing about them, except that I was pulled to them like a magnetic force. I was smitten. My mother did not grow herbs in her garden when I was growing up, so I had not been introduced to them before, but I feel I have known about them forever, perhaps from a past life. I wanted to learn more about these lovely plants that I was attracted to.

Many years ago when I purchased my first herb, a lavender plant, there was not much information available on herbs. This was in the days before the Internet. I found a book or two touting the culinary attributes of various herbs like lavender, sage, rosemary and thyme, or telling how to make a potpourri from them. And they all smelled divine – a little like the sun and a little like the earth. Magical.

Most of the herbs I planted thrived in my midwestern garden, and I delighted in rubbing their leaves and asking them to reveal their secrets. I used them in making potpourri at first, and then I started using them in cooking and baking. But something was missing. Little by little the secrets emerged. Medicine. Plant medicine – people medicine.

Soon I was taking a journey down an unknown path to learn about the medicine of these plants and what they could do for the health of my family and me. And later the Internet and more books became available and opened up a whole new world that I had thirsted for and now could not turn back from – ever. It was in my genes from a long way back in history, as my ancestral grand-mothers had to know about these plants to keep their families healthy.

I learned to make tinctures for medicine, infused vinegars for health, oil infusions to make "lotions and potions," and more. I loved learning the basics of natural medicine and what the plants could teach, and teach me they did – as they still do every day of my life.

Today, my daughter and I teach a 10-month *Home Herbalism* course to help others learn what it took me years and years to learn. And I am still learning. The plants are still calling to me and teaching me their secrets. I am listening.

Candle ring made from fresh lamb's ear and chive flowers

RHUBARB

*L*OVE IT OR HATE IT

I love rhubarb! But I did not love rhubarb to begin with.

I truly believe those who hate rhubarb will love it if it is cooked and baked correctly – or perhaps we just grow into loving it.

Rhubarb is the first fruit of spring, but it is technically a vegetable, functioning like a fruit – and it is also an herb, which means it is a plant that is useful. Since the introduction of sugar to sweeten the rhubarb and make it more palatable, it became widely grown. Adding a sweetener to rhubarb makes a mix of tart and sweet, and with a scoop of vanilla ice cream it becomes a "food of the gods."

Rhubarb seems to be a mystery plant to many people with it being fruit, vegetable and herb. It is all three, but we use it mainly as a dessert plant. Most of us know it as the "common pie plant," and it makes delicious pies. People either love it or hate it and there does not seem to be any in-between feeling about it. My hubby loved it and I did not. But as time went on and I made him rhubarb desserts every spring, he would rave over them, and I grew to appreciate it also, and now believe it to be quite a delicacy.

In fact, my garden cannot be without rhubarb now. It looks more like a "show-off" landscape plant than anything else because of its huge leaves and red stalks. Only the stalks are consumed, and I have found a use for the huge leaves that are poisonous to humans. I use the leaves to make cement birdbaths molded around the biggest leaves of the rhubarb plant.

My rhubarb was a pass-along plant from friend Shirley when we moved from Colorado back home to the prairies of Nebraska. Originally I had planted the rhubarb in a nice place, or so I thought at the time, but then the shrubs and iris grew taller and shaded the rhubarb too much – rhubarb needs sunshine to grow. I transplanted three hills into five. A rhubarb plant can be separated out, usually with the help of a spade or big knife, so each new start has at least two "eyes" on the new crown plant.

I watch anxiously each early spring for the rhubarb to emerge from the earth, as I know I must see it first before the wild creatures do or they will eat it off continuously. I anchor a mesh cover to the earth, letting the sunshine in but protecting the delicate new leaves.

Rhubarb is an old-fashioned plant, and I wonder if people will grow rhubarb at all in the future. Generations change, tastes change, and if children are not exposed to it, most certainly it will not be grown. And now, many people either eat out or buy packaged food instead of baking or cooking in the home. I love the process of making and baking, the aroma coming from the oven on a mild day near the end of April, and then the delectable flavor when savoring a bite of warm rhubarb dessert. Simple pleasures.

I use rhubarb in desserts every spring and make rhubarb-strawberry jam for the grandsons, so perhaps one day I can pass along a start of rhubarb to their gardens. It is a faithful plant and will grow for many years. When I travel the back roads and see an abandoned farmstead, I always smile when I see the daffodils, lilacs and the rhubarb in the springtime. I think of the old farm women, the grandmothers, who planted the rhubarb a long time ago and how it fed the bodies and souls of those who worked so hard. Rhubarb recipes have been passed down through the generations, and rhubarb will always have a place of honor in my garden for all the delicious springtime memories it gives us.

RHUBARB CAN BE PURCHASED AT SOME GARDEN centers, or ask to dig an old plant or part of an old plant from a friend who will share with you. This delicacy is expensive in the grocery store and at farmers markets – if you can even find it there. At my farmers market it is sold out within fifteen minutes, as it is very much sought after by home cooks in the spring. It is an easy-to-grow, low-maintenance plant. I plant it and forget it, other than watering once in a while during a very dry summer or covering from the wild creatures in the early spring. I keep the weeds down around the rhubarb with some organic mulch (natural only, never dyed colors) or their own leaves when a stem is pulled. My rhubarb likes some organic matter like old dried leaves or a little compost or rotted manure. Rhubarb really asks for very little and gives so much back. My mom's wise words were that the *red* stalked rhubarb is the best – prettier when cooked, and perhaps not quite as tart as the green-stemmed rhubarb, thus requiring less sugar. I remember the names of *Victoria* and *Canada Red* as being two good old varieties to plant with red stalks.

RHUBARB GROWS WILD IN CHINA AND TIBET AND IS used in medicines there. In the 1700's it was introduced to the United States and became very popular as a hardy perennial and soon was offered in markets. Rhubarb is a member of the buck-wheat family and a close cousin of the wild plant called sorrel. The plant goes dormant in the winter here in the Midwest and produces its edible stems in the spring. Medicinally and tradition-ally, the rhizomes were used dried and powdered as a tonic for digestion, a mild laxative and general healing of wounds and burns.

My mama told me not to harvest a new rhubarb plant for two years and then only take two stalks. The third year half the plant can be harvested. I also remember the old saying about growing perennials:

The first year they sleep,
the second year they creep
and the third year they leap.

There are different opinions on whether one should snap the stem by wiggling and pulling or cut it off at the ground with a knife. Pulling or snapping is the way I was taught. I harvest part of the plant now and allow the rest to feed and produce more stems to grow a bigger plant next year. Once the stem bolts (goes to flower), I immediately clip the flowers off daily, as this allows the stems to keep producing into the early summer. I find the very hot days around the end of May make the stalks tougher. Harvesting begins in April and goes through May where I live. I use some stalks fresh, making into desserts and jam and freeze the rest. After washing and towel-drying the stalks, I cut into one-inch pieces and dry pack, which means nothing added. I freeze in two to four-cup bags pre-measured for future recipes and double bag to freeze. If using fresh, rhubarb will keep for two weeks in a sealed bag in refrigerator, but it is always better if used as soon as possible. When I am ready to use it, I cut a small piece off the bottom of the stalk, stand it in water to freshen and use an hour later.

Eating rhubarb from the garden made into desserts or jam is a springtime family tradition – one we greatly anticipate each year. Many rhubarb recipes include another spring favorite – strawberries. They enhance each other. I believe it is important to eat in season, but I also preserve for eating later on.

Caution: Do not eat rhubarb leaves, as they are poisonous.

SPRINGTIME AND THE WILD PLUM THICKETS

The windows are open on this beautiful early spring day, and the delicate fragrance wafting through I immediately recognize as coming from the wild plum thicket to the south of my country home. The wild native plum blossoms are another harbinger of spring. It is the time when the windows can finally opened, the grass will need mowing, and the garden can be planted.

Wild plum thickets grow along the country roads and are a common sight in the midwestern states. I am sure many people driving quickly to their destination will not look twice at the plum thickets, but I slow down and look for them, and then I stop to gaze at the beauty of Mother Nature. Seeking out the blooming wild plum thickets is an annual springtime ritual for me.

In the spring, my kitchen island or farm table will be graced with a bouquet of the blooming branches, and my home is perfumed with their intoxicating fragrance – not too heady but just right. I look at the delicate little blossoms and marvel at their individual beauty. In early spring I keep a watchful eye for the first showy white cloud of flowers on the horizon indicating a large patch of wild plums in full bloom. Often my dear hubby would find a patch blooming before I did and bring me the first bouquet.

The blooms are fleeting, lasting about a week, and a spring frost will turn them brown overnight. As I would drive by a thicket often, I would watch as the creamy petals would drop and the little green leaves would appear. Soon the bushes were a mass of green. Come early summer, as soon as the field thistles created their fluffy seed heads, the finches would gather the fluff to line their nests in the plum thickets. Come early fall, I would start watching to see if this was a year for the plums to have a good crop, as many years they don't.

When the fruits turn a dark orange-ruby red indicating ripeness, I would start picking, taking only enough for jam and leaving the rest for the birds. Tasting a fruit would usually leave my mouth puckered and face in a big frown, as the fruit is quite tart. After picking a couple gallons of the largest fruit, I would bring them home to wash and make into jelly.

I am thinking it is time that I plant my own wild plum thicket as a place that can be enjoyed by my grandchildren too one day. We all need a place to feed our body and spirit when the world becomes a bit too hectic around us.

LILACS

THE FRAGRANCE OF SPRING

I want to have a little house
with sunlight on the floors,
A chimney with a rosy hearth,
and lilacs by the door,
With windows looking east and west,
and a crooked apple tree
And room beside the garden fence
for hollyhocks to be.
-N.B. Turner

There are heart-singing moments when I walk through my garden in spring. I am intoxicated by the fragrance on the whiffs of wind that brush past me, and the most intoxicating of all is the fragrance of an old-fashioned lilac.

Many years ago, it has been said, the lilac was planted close to a home to keep evil away. Supposedly, the fragrance alone would keep away ghosts. The beauty and fragrance of the lilac beckons me come linger awhile and to lose myself in the mysteries of this shrub.

L'ilas

The old-fashioned lilac now blooms mid- to late-April here in the Midwest. The common lilac is the most aromatic of all to me. Hybrids I planted turned out to be beautiful to look at, but completely lacked substance as they barely had any fragrance compared to the common lilac.

Lilacs today come in many colors and can be grown worldwide, especially in the northern climates, as lilacs need a period of rest in winter to do well.

One can almost always find a lilac bush on an old abandoned farmstead. Lilacs are easy to share as pass-along plants, as a small shoot can be dug up from the mother lilac. I feel every home should have a lilac growing in the yard for its beauty and fragrance. Lilacs are an unforgettable spring blessing.

Still grows the vivacious lilac
a generation after the door and lintel
and the sill are gone,
unfolding its sweet-scented flowers
each spring.
–Henry David Thoreau

VIOLETS

Unlike many wildflowers, the violet is not harmed by picking its blossoms, for these showy flowers seldom or never produce seed anyway. Apparently, they are produced out of sheer exuberance, so take all of them if you want, for the more you pick the more the plant will give.
-Euell Gibbons

esterday I picked violet flowers. They grow in abundance on the edge of the woods where I live, receiving enough sunlight to give them energy to grow and enough shade for a little relief from the strong rays of sun. The violet is a wonderful wild garden and prairie flower, and depending on where located, they will bloom from March to the end of May.

Violets are quite aggressive little flowers, but I don't mind as there is plenty of room in the meadows and woodlands for them to grow, and I adore their little flower — it seems there are no two alike. I find light blue, then a dark blue, and then a mixture of both colors and so on. This diminutive little flower is a delight to behold — and is also edible. I like to add violet flowers to the top of a serving of strawberry shortcake, a mini white frosted cupcake or a serving of chicken salad.

I collect the flowers for dessert in the evening, as the flowers will not last long once picked. The tender young leaves are also good chopped up into a greens salad, but the leaves need to be eaten in early spring before they get old and tough. They can be eaten like spinach, but should be eaten a little sparingly at first, as too big a serving can act like a laxative. The violet leaf is nutritious, and that is why I add it to my salads when I can. It has lots of Vitamins A and C and iron.

Euell Gibbons called the violet *nature's vitamin pill*. Scientists today have found that the violet plant does indeed contain healing compounds. Traditionally for medicine, a cough syrup can be made from the young leaves, and also tea can be made from fresh leaves for urinary infections. Our ancestors would use it as an ointment for rheumatism. Because of its heart shaped leaves it was believed to be good for the heart also. This is an impressive little plant that many call a "weed."

I love freezing violet flowers (or other edible flowers) in ice cubes. I add the ice cubes to a glass of fresh lemon balm and mint-infused water as a refreshing drink for my guests. My method: fill ice cube tray one-third full and freeze. Then add a violet flower in the middle and add a bit of water. Freeze. When frozen, fill the rest of the way with water and freeze. The violet flower stays frozen in the middle. Guests will be impressed.

The violet is also called the *fairy flower* as folklore says the fairies get out their paintbrushes in the spring and paint each flower, and that is why there are different colors.

Violets are a member of the viola family, which also includes

Johnny jump-ups, violas, and pansies, and all have been called by the old country name of *hearts-ease*. Violets do not produce seed from the first spring flowers, but will make seed in the late summer from a hidden flower, giving a little mystery to this plant. It also spreads moderately from underground runners.

A simple syrup can be made from violet flowers. Fresh flowers and leaves can also be tinctured. Native Americans collected the small violet bulbs, then boiled and dried them to store for winter food. Violet jelly is delicious and makes a wonderful jewel-toned jelly.

The ancestors say that one should grow violets by the doorstep as it offers protection and easing of heart pain. I have violets growing by my front doorstep – they planted themselves, or perhaps had some help from the fairies.

Collecting the flowers and leaves of this tiny plant can be time consuming. I find a patch and sit in the middle, collecting all around me, and then move to another patch. I sing to the plants as I ask for permission to collect their flowers. I consider these little beauties to be my herbal friends for the many benefits they give.

Who bends a knee where violets grow –
a hundred secret things shall know.
-Rachel Field

VIOLET TEA
The hot tea is good for a sore throat and when cooled down can also be used on a rash, as a mouthwash for sore gums or a gargle.
1 handful of violet leaves, washed and chopped
1 c. hot water and steep

VIOLET VINEGAR
Fill a pint jar (or half pint jar) with violet flowers. Do not wash (if it rains, wait a day or two before collecting). Pour plain white *wine* vinegar over the flowers. Use a non-metal lid, as vinegar will corrode metal. Let sit for 10 days, strain and refrigerate. Can be used in a salad dressing with olive oil.

THE AMAZING DANDY-LION

THE KING OF WEEDS

A weed is a plant whose virtues have not yet been discovered.
-Emerson

I NEVER KNEW!

I remember when my children were little they delighted in bringing me a small bouquet of freshly picked bright dandelion flowers. As years passed, a grandchild would pick a dandelion and carefully bring it into the house to give to me – beautiful gifts from precious givers.

And do you remember blowing on the fluffy seed heads as a child and watching them scatter in the wind? Or making a necklace chain from the flower stalks and your hands would get sticky from the milky sap? Oh, to be a child and see the beauty around us as a child sees it – without judgment!

Knowing what I know today about the humble sweet yellow dandelion, I am wondering how anyone can call it a weed and try to kill it. *I never knew!* I didn't know that this so-called weed could actually be good for a person. If people knew about its goodness, they would not be attacking dandelions in lawns with chemicals every year, trying to make lawns look "picture perfect" when they are anything but perfect – lawns today are so full of chemicals that warnings are given to not let children or animals walk on them. That *should* tell us something!

"The dandelion is one of the most complete foods on earth," says noted herbalist Gregory Tilford. The Latin name for dandelion is *Taraxacum officinale* which means *official remedy for disorders.*

Sometime ago, I discovered a book of 100 pages written on dandelion alone, with recipes for muffins, cookies, wine and beer, ointments and salves, and more. The book is called *Dandelion Medicine* by Brigitte Mars. I was curious, so I read the book and developed a great respect for the dandelion. What I might have thought was a plant food for my great-grandmother's generation or poor people is actually a plant food held in high esteem and can now be found for sale in health food stores.

Today I make a healing salve from dandelion, and enjoy cookies, a cup of dandelion tea and young leaves in my salad – all from this magnificent weed we call dandelion. Before the plant flowers in very early spring, I am collecting and drying the abundant new spring leaves. The leaves dry on a clean white cotton dishtowel on my big island in the kitchen and when thoroughly dry I store them in an airtight half-gallon jar. When I need to use them in winter I will crumble them and add to a soup or omelet for an added nutritional boost. Otherwise, I use fresh when I can.

Everything and more I wanted to learn about one of my now-favorite wild spring herbs, the dandelion, is in the *Dandelion Medicine* book — a wonderful, easy read full of great information. Here are a few more important facts about Dandelion:

— Early spring is the best time to pick dandelion leaves, as they are most tender and mild

— Older leaves can be bitter, so pick from the center new leaves, not outer-edge older leaves

— Dandelion coffee is made from dried and roasted root, cut in pieces and ground

— Roots are a liver tonic and should be dug in the fall when the nutrients go back down below ground into the root

— The milky white sap from the flower stalk is said to remove warts

— Wool cloth/yarn can be dyed from the roots and flowers, making a soft yellow/green color

NOTE: *Avoid picking ANY edible weed where chemical fertilizers/herbicides have been used in last three years.*

IN THE SPRING, WHEN THE MEADOW NEARBY IS FULL OF sweet dandelion flowers and the bees feed on their first food after the long winter, I believe there is a universal plan – a reason as to why the dandelions grow so prolifically. The plant is meant to be abundant to us as food for our body and soul. It is a bright yellow color to call attention to it so we notice it and don't destroy it. The dandelion is truly a magical gift from Mother Earth.

I kept a yellow dandelion,
For I liked to watch it grow
And I could never understand
Why people hate them so!
I cared for my dandelion
Until it was old and gray
And along came a puff of wind
And blew his hair away.
-unknown

DANDELION FLOWER COOKIES

1 stick butter, softened
1/2 c. honey
2 eggs
1 tsp. vanilla extract
1 c. flour
1 c. oatmeal, in blender or processor to make it like coarse flour
1/2 c. dandelion yellow petals, green calyx part removed

Gather dandelion flowers from unsprayed area (and where pets do not roam). Hold the calyx (green part) firmly with thumb and finger of one hand and pull out the yellow dandelion petals with the other hand. Throw away the green part, as it can be bitter. Mix butter and honey together, add eggs and vanilla, and then the dried ingredients. Drop by teaspoonful on parchment paper lined cookie sheet. Bake at 350 for 10-15 minutes, watching carefully until the edges start to crisp. Remove immediately from the oven and let cool before removing from cookie sheet. Makes 2 dozen cookies.

(Adapted from *Dandelion Medicine* by Brigitte Mars)

ARBOR DAY

He that plants a tree loves others besides himself.
-Thomas Fuller

ARBOR DAY was founded in 1872 by Julius Sterling Morton in Nebraska City, Nebraska. I grew up in Nebraska, and on Arbor Day many school age children had to write reports about this important day and many field trips were planned to visit his historical home and the grounds around it.

Planting a tree is another way to green up America, as well as to help purify the air we breathe, as trees give off oxygen. Whenever we planted a tree – and we have planted many on different acreages we lived on – my mom would always ask us, without fail, "what kind of tree did we plant?" Living through the depression, her thoughts were that a tree needed to produce food first and foremost, and a fruit tree or nut tree would give us food throughout the years ahead. I understood that philosophy well, and my hubby and I planted many fruit trees. We also planted shelterbelts of trees along the perimeter of our acreage to break the wind in the winter and shade trees to shelter our home on a hot summer day. So, as soon as I moved into my home in the woods, I found a clearing large enough to plant a *Liberty* apple tree. One day I am hopeful someone else will appreciate this apple tree and the fruit it bears.

Someone is sitting in the shade today
because someone planted a tree
a long time ago.
-Warren Buffett

EARTH DAY

I pledge allegiance to the Earth,
and to the flora, fauna and human life that it supports,
One planet, indivisible,
with safe air, water and soil,
economic justice, equal rights
and: Peace for all.
-Women's Environment & Development Organization of the
Women's Foreign Policy Council

*E*arth Day is one of our recognized special days brought about to create awareness for taking care of our planet – our home. It is vitally important that we start NOW for our children's children and the generations to come. It is the responsibility of our schools, parents and grandparents, and the community to teach the children to save what we have, to not waste it, and to protect it.

EARTH DAY was started April 22, 1970, as a day to celebrate and appreciate Mother Earth. It is sad we need to be reminded to care for her each day. My hope is that one day everything can be recycled. I am reminded of what my mom used to say to me and my five siblings many times as we were growing up: *"Use it up, wear it out, make it do, or do without."* I am sure she probably heard it many times from her own mother as well.

RACHEL CARSON MADE ME aware of the earth around me when I read her book, *The Silent Spring*, in the late 60's. I was deeply touched by this nature-loving woman who wanted to change the world's thinking. Many of her predictions are coming to pass. Now there is a children's book called *Rachel: The Story of Rachel Carson* for the younger children to read. We teach little people about nature and preserving it so one day they can carry on the legacy. I feel it is important to be inspired by nature at a very early age by taking the children to a city or state park or walking around the neighborhood looking at the trees, the plants and the insects. Hug a tree. Children love learning.

The butterflies and bees are disappearing, and I notice fewer each year where I live. The endangered species list is growing. What is happening? Will they all disappear? I believe the birds, butterflies and insects are dying from the use of herbicides and pesticides, and the clearing of so much habitat where the animals and birds live. It all plays a big ugly part in the health of the natural world, which includes all of us — the human species.

The most common form of terrorism in the U.S.A. is that which is carried on by bulldozers and chainsaws. It is not enough to understand the natural world; the point is to defend and preserve it. Sentiment without action is the ruin of the soul.
-Edward Abbey, 1927-1989

As long as I am able, I will grow many of my own organic vegetables and buy locally produced meat and homegrown items at the local Farmer's Market. When we buy from a grocery store it is important to understand that many of the items we eat have to be trucked in from a thousand miles or more away, and that adds to the cost of what we buy, as well as putting fumes in the air and consumption of fuel to run the trucks. Buying from a CSA or creating a food co-op in our area is another good idea.

One of the most important resources that a garden makes available is the gardener's own body. A garden gives the body the dignity of working in its own support. It is a way of rejoining the human race.
-Wendell Berry

MY PARENTS GREW UP DURING THE DEPRESSION knowing they could not waste anything. And those frugal traits were passed on. We did not waste food on our plates — we took only what we could eat and ate it all. We never wasted a drop of water, as we had to haul water to the house. Our clothes were hand-me-downs. Money was used wisely and sparingly and was saved to buy what was needed. There were no credit cards then. We always had a garden and canned the fruits and vegetables to get us through the long winter months, and we were good stewards of the land.

The elders have spoken.
Just as we use the land to heal ourselves,
we must in return heal the land.
-Native American saying

My hope and prayer is that children today are taught this. I believe it is our responsibility as residents on this earth to help preserve this land that gives to us so abundantly. I pray we will not abuse her and everyone can be an earth keeper – not just on Earth Day.

This we know. The earth does not belong to man;
man belongs to the earth.
All things are connected
like the blood which unites one family.
All things are connected:
Whatever befalls the earth
befalls the sons of the earth.
Man did not weave the web of life;
he is merely a strand in it.
Whatever he does to the web,
he does to himself.
-Chief Seattle

Wild blue flax

PASS-ALONG

❦

NOT ONLY A SIGN OF FRUGALITY – BUT OF FRIENDSHIP

There are *pass-along* plants, *pass-along* clothes, *pass-along* recipes and *pass-along* – well, almost everything. *Pass-along* means to share or give away, and I love this sentiment.

I was raised in a frugal home with few extras in life when I was growing up. Being raised in a farming community, I was not a fashion-conscious person, and it would not have mattered if I was. Many times, my pass-along clothing came from my older cousin Irene, and as a teenager I did not care for her style of clothing. It was not MY style, if anything could really be called "my style" at that time. I did not like pass-along clothes at all – the style, or the color or how it looked on me – but I wore it anyway, as there was not much else to choose from. It was a time when clothes were handed down to others often without a second thought. Clothes today are usually not passed along – they are thrown away. Today I believe that *pass-along* or recycled is a good idea indeed.

There was a time when much of the food I cooked came from *pass-along* recipes shared by many good cooks from my family and friends. I still find myself collecting recipes from other people. When I attend a function or group and taste something I like, I am soon searching out the cook to ask if they would share the recipe and "pass it along" to me. Many times, they will say, "Oh, that is my sister's recipe" or someone else's recipe, one that was passed along to them, and we then become collectors of *pass-along* recipes without realizing it. Some of my best recipes have come to me that way. In turn, I freely pass along a recipe when someone asks.

When I moved back to the plains of Nebraska from the high-altitude mountains of Colorado, I knew I needed some *pass-along* plants to get me started gardening on the prairie again. I put the word out and asked for help from anyone cleaning out their gardens or who could spare a plant. The first plants I received were three rhubarb plants from friend Shirley, who shared some of her mom's garden with me. And now in my Kansas garden I have multiple *pass-along* plants given to me by new friends.

My mom gave me a few of Great-Grandma's little miniature iris as *pass-along* plants. These have been carefully tended, divided and passed along for many years.

My life is richer today because of something being passed along to me. I am still not a fashion-conscious person, my cooking and baking will not win awards, and my gardens will not appear on the glossy pages of a garden magazine, but I enjoy the things passed along, like the *pass-along* clothing, recipes and plants which have helped shape my values.

Pass-along is something that never goes out of style. In this complicated world we live in today, much joy comes from picking the spring stalks of Shirley's mom's rhubarb, making the rhubarb dessert from a pass-along recipe of Aunt Maxine's, or seeing the stonecrop growing in my new garden from friend Nancy. The world is a better place because we shared and something was passed along to us or we passed along something to someone else. I want to always share and *pass-along* to others – it makes the world a much more loving and interesting place to live.

May

THE VIEW FROM MY WINDOW

The world's favorite season is the spring.
All things seem possible in May.
-Edwin Way

It's a beautiful day in my neighborhood. –Mr. Rogers

As I sit this morning in my vine-covered screened-in porch listening to the birds singing, I think of the words of Mr. Rogers, from kids' TV fame. He would sing, "It's a beautiful day in my neighborhood," perhaps a little off key, but still such soothing words. When the grandkids would stay overnight I would greet them in the morning with this song and they would smile, instantly taking away any grumpiness.

It really is a beautiful May Day in my neighborhood, as two inches of rain fell to the earth last night, keeping everything growing and very green. The air is fresh and the birds are singing non-stop, keeping me company as I drink my cup of hot tea. The bullfrog that lives under the coolness of the silver lace vine by the porch is *ribbiting* his *good morning* also.

I saw an act of faith today —
A man was on his knees
Not in a pew in church,
But in a garden planting seeds
-Unknown

In this merry month of May, I am looking forward to planting the rest of the garden. Many of us who live in the Midwest or northern central states look forward to this joyous month with anticipation every year. The weather is nicer, the rest of the veggies and flowers can be planted, many perennial flowers are blooming, and it is the end of the school year for children and graduation celebrations are planned. But most of all, I love being in the garden planting seeds and watching them grow. I am reminded of this quote every spring:

My soul requires that I garden – it is just necessary.
-Frances Parker

There are surprises everywhere on these May days. Driving up my long country lane in May, I see vistas of springtime everywhere. The neighbor's wheat field is a beautiful spring green color. The crab apple trees have bloomed, and the many tulip bulbs I planted last fall are winding down with their bursts of color here and there. The peach tree, planted from the seed of an old-fashioned white peach, is now fifteen-feet tall and covered in pink blossoms.

My son stopped by on this May Day and said, "Take a walk with me." I never miss an opportunity to spend a few extra moments with my kids and grandkids. We walked over to the old north garden and there were at least a dozen five-foot tall stalks in full bloom — a bright pink. The little trees were spaced no more than eight inches apart.

Now the thing is, this is right next to the curve in my lane and the day before they were NOT blooming, or I would have noticed them, nor had I ever seen them before. My son wanted me to iden-tify the blooming twigs, and one look told me they were the old-fashioned white peach. Evidently they had grown from peach pits I had thrown out into the old compost pile a few years ago. I had been throwing compost-like materials on that pile for ten years or more. The peach trees are heirloom trees with the sweetest fruit ever – a true delicacy. So, son and a friend dug up the trees and transplanted them to their homes. If these trees had not been blooming we would never have noticed them at all. Nature has a way of saying, *look at me – here I am*. The big mother peach tree is close to my house and never fails to bloom and produce. Mother Nature is full of surprises.

Alas, the deer have discovered all the gourmet food around my home this time of year, and they have proceeded to munch every single bloom off the tulips overnight. I was enjoying the blooms on the many tulips I had planted the autumn before – especially the Tasha Tudor favored one called *Apricot Beauty*. I really did not think they would eat them this close to my home. And to add insult to injury, they bit off the tulip blooms and spit them out, deciding they weren't as tasty as they looked. The deer must have been hungry – they left their hoof prints all over, telling me exactly who the culprits were.

During the winter months I can look at the neighbor's snow-covered field with the creek in the distance and count over a dozen deer at any one time, so I know they live close to my home, sheltered by the trees along the edge of the creek. Right now, I don't feel they are being real neighborly with their actions, but we all live in the same world under the same moon.

THE IRIS ARE IN FULL BLOOM IN MY GARDEN. THIS flower was — and still is — called *the poor man's orchid*. I love the iris flower as my mother, her mother and my great grandmother did. And now my daughter has gorgeous hybrid iris growing in her garden, as well as the old-fashioned varieties. My mom's favorites she planted years ago were called *Easter Bonnet*, *Babbling Brook* and *Stepping Out*. I wonder which ones will become my favorites in time and my daughter's favorites. We both love the one called *Dusky Challenger* – a dark purple velvety large hybrid iris. I also like one called *Batik*.

The colors on the iris are spectacular, and I check each morning to see what is blooming. I take pictures, but there is no comparison to seeing the iris in its full glorious bloom. Mother Nature's brushes have painted exquisite colors on my flowers this spring.

Where flowers bloom, so does hope.
–Eleanor Roosevelt

The lilacs usually bloom close to Mother's Day in mid-May depending on the year. With global warming they are in full bloom by May 1st, having begun blooming the end of April. I always pick a few stems to bring inside to enjoy as long as I can. The scent is elusive. I have read it is almost impossible to capture this scent naturally, so we must enjoy them when they bloom. Although lilac-scented candles and soaps have been made synthetically, humans cannot improve on Mother Nature. My lilacs are the old-fashioned kind – a *pass-along* plant from a friend. The bloom and scent of the lilac is fleeting, so I take time to smell the flowers when they are blooming.

May Baskets are made for the first day of May, called *May Day*. This has become a lost tradition, and May 1st has become just another day to many people. I believe making May baskets is a lovely old custom that needs reviving in this hectic and busy world we live in. When I was a child we would make May baskets from construction paper or a paper cup with bits of lace and paper flowers glued on. Inside the May basket we would add a petunia and some candy, and if we could not buy the petunia, a dandelion picked out of the yard would do. After making them, the baskets would be delivered to a friend, neighbor or relative. A May basket is as much fun to give as to receive.

When my niece was married on May Day some years ago, my large family of brothers and sisters, spouses, grandchildren and grandparents, attended the Kansas City wedding. Unbeknownst to us, my sister Linda made May baskets, and very early on May Day morning delivered them with a surprise knock on our hotel door. The tradition is to leave the basket by the door and hide so the recipient would not know who left the May basket, but we soon solved the mystery. The May basket she created was made from an old small square wooden strawberry box, the kind that fresh strawberries used to be purchased in before plastic. She glued wide ribbon around the rim and created a handle from the ribbon. Inside the May basket was a pretty pansy plant and individually wrapped candies. The wedding weekend was made more special by the unexpected surprise of May baskets. Memories like this stay with us, and many years later we still talk about the May Day basket surprise.

The birds are busy this May. Papa and Mama Bluebird are camped out in an old green painted birdhouse attached to the top of the log double swing, six feet from the door of the screened-in porch. I have a good view of them as mama and papa are resting nearby watching over their surroundings. The silver lace vine almost covered the birdhouse last year, so this year I trimmed it back early to make it easier for the birds to find their home, and for me to view it as well. The birds still have a hidden place to nest. Mama is a drab gray color, but proud papa bluebird is striking in his sky-blue suit.

The wrens, with their happy spring song, have chosen an antique birdhouse by the shop's door and now call it "Home Sweet Home." Needless to say, I won't be selling that birdhouse at the shop until this family vacates.

House finches, with the male having a reddish head, have decided to nest nearby, making their home in a grapevine wreath hanging on the porch. The nest sits a little precariously on some dried vines protected from the elements by the eaves. It is in a fine spot, shaded and out of the wind and rain, and mama finch does not seem to mind my comings and goings.

Mama Robin has built her nest right under the grape arbor that covers the top of my big window. She is easy to see, and I stand back, not wanting to disturb her "secret" place to nest.

I see a pair of mourning doves *cooing* to each other close by, making me think they are more "lovebirds" than doves. Later in the afternoon I discover their nest in the honeysuckle vine on the opposite side of the log double swing. They are neighbors to the bluebirds on the opposite end.

Wild turkeys have been *gobbling* in the woods. The turkeys have walked to the edge of the backyard, across the narrow field from the creek, where the "king" of the flock fluffed up his fantail feathers and put on quite a show. I was mesmerized by him, and I wondered if his flock of ladies felt the same way.

The friendly quail eat the birdseed where it falls from the feeders, and I believe the quail are nesting close by, as I hear them each morning with their distinct *bob white* call. The feeding station with food and water has made my bird friends feel welcome close to where I live.

In May the Farmers' Market reopens, and visiting local growers is always a treat. Going to Farmers' Market has become a weekend ritual for me in the spring. I take a gathering basket and check out the many vendors, buying items I need that I don't grow or are not ready in my own garden yet. I always patronize the farmers who do not use chemicals (pesticides, herbicides, chemical fertilizers).

This is healthy food — the kind of food I grew up on many years ago on the farm. Back then we just called it *food*, but today we have to seek it out as *organic* food. Chemicals are not good for earth or its creatures – including us.

The Farmers' Market is a *happening* event. It is a neat place, with the sights, sounds and smells of good food and musical entertainment. I buy fresh lettuce and spinach greens from a favorite vendor, potted herb plants including orange-scented thyme I have never seen before, and grass-fed beef, and then I head home with my treasures. I am a firm believer in growing our own food if possible, or at least growing some of our food and buying and eating the rest locally.

Bless the farmers who raise the food organically without chemicals for the bees and me, and protect the earth while doing so. And bless my father who was a farmer, so I could grow up in the country and learn to love the wild plants, trees, cows and chickens. And bless my mother, a farmer's wife, for having a big garden and preserving the food, which makes me conscious of what I eat today.

> *Mother's Day is a thank you card to every woman who has ever hugged a baby, kissed a boo-boo, listened closely, cared deeply – and passed on her love and wisdom to others who needed her too.*
> -Unknown

I am grateful to the woman who birthed me and all the women along the way who have nurtured me through all these years. There were many, and I needed every one of them at one time or another — strong women and good friends.

Happy Mother's Day.

THE FULL MOON IN MAY

*N*ative Americans, as well as others who came before us, had several names for the full moon in the month of May to keep track of time before calendars. When it was time to plant the garden or when they planted their crops long ago, or when the storms filled the skies and when the flowers were blooming across the land, they named the May Full Moon.

Full Flower Moon was named in May, as all the plants seem to be blooming at that time. Everywhere the prairies, meadows and gardens are colorful and fragrant. How appropriate these wonderful names were given to the month's full moon to identify this time of year.

Storms Full Moon could also be called *Raging Sky Full Moon* if I were to name it. I understand the *Storms Full Moon* very well living in the Midwest, as many storms gear up in April to make their presence known in the month of May. This is the month of booming thunderstorms with torrential rain, high winds, and sometimes hail and tornadoes.

Planting Full Moon is for those of us on our knees on the earth planting gardens, and also the farmers tilling the earth in the fields, planting the crops of oats, soybeans and corn.

The wise old women, our grandmothers, taught us to never plant on the day of the full moon, but to rest. Also, to watch carefully the waxing and waning of the moon, the increasing and decreasing light, and the gravitational pull of the moon energy, which affects every living thing. This sage advice was passed down through the generations, and I remember it as I plant my garden in this *Planting Moon* season. When talking to my mom, now in her 90's, and telling her I was planting my garden, she would ask me, as she did each year, *"Was it the right sign of the moon?"* To many this is viewed as myth and folklore, but there is actually research and truth in it. We were taught to plant seeds from the dark of the moon to the full moon. And then harvest (dry and preserve) from full moon back to the dark, which is the new moon.

At new moon, or no moonlight, the lunar gravity begins to pull water up and cause the seeds to swell and burst open. The increasing moonlight creates balanced root and leaf growth. It is the best time to plant above ground annual crops like beans, spinach, lettuce, and other above-ground producing food. In the second quarter, half-dark and half-light, the gravity pull is less, but the moonlight is still strong enough to create leaf growth to establish strong plants, so I plant the vining plants like squash, cucumbers, and also tomatoes.

After the full moon, as it is waning, the energy draws down and creates more moisture in the earth. The moonlight is decreasing, putting energy into roots, so it is a good time to plant perennials and root crops like beets, turnips, onions, carrots and potatoes. In the third quarter of the moon it is time for pruning and propagating. The fourth quarter is a resting period for plants, a time to cultivate and harvest.

Lunar signs are fun to read about, and I've learned from several sources. Many wall calendars show the moon signs as well. The oldest available print source of moon signs is the *Farmer's Almanac*, which has been printed since the late 1800's.

FULL MOON TEA

Making *Full Moon Tea* is both delicious and magical.

Here is my method: Gather herbs. I like a handful of lemon balm, a sprig or two of spearmint, and maybe a few rose petals or a lavender flower stem *(rose and lavender are quite strong and I have learned a little can go a long ways)*. I make what is technically a infusion, but we call it a tea, as most understand this word better. It is a very refreshing beverage on a hot summer day, and guests love it!

I put the herbs in a half-gallon jar, add purified water to it, cover with the lid and place it on the earth at dusk to sit all night under the rays of the full moon. The moonbeams are full of magic and energy – a good time to make moon tea. The next morning I bring it inside, strain out the herbs and put it in the refrigerator to drink over the next two days.

Tip: *The tea is good for two days. The leftover tea can be frozen into ice cubes or used to water plants. The "used up herbs" can be thrown on the compost pile.*

I make *Full Moon Tea* any of the nights of the full moon, which include the night before the full moon, the night of and the night after the full moon, as all three nights of the full moon are magical.

When the grandchildren were little, we would dance in the light of the full moon singing songs – especially *I see the moon and the moon sees me* and the words to *Moon, Sister Moon*. Hopefully one day my grandchildren and their grandchildren will dance and sing in the light of the full moon and make *Full Moon Tea* from the herbs of the earth.

IN THE GARDEN IN MAY

And spring arose on the garden fair,
Like the Spring of Love felt everywhere;
And each flower and herb on Earth's dark breast,
Arose from the dreams of the wintry rest.
-Percy Bysshe Shelley

*M*ay is a grand month in the garden. With global warming, everything blooms a little earlier by at least two weeks. May finds the larkspur ready to bloom and the iris in full bloom. It has been "show time" in my *wild woman* yard and garden. Sometimes I feel there is no rhyme or reason to my yard, so I call it *wild*. I like it all – wherever it pops up. I let plants live where they choose most of the time. I like to think there is structure in my life, but there seems to be none in my garden!

Around Mother's Day in the middle of May is the best time of all in the garden. The weather is usually not too hot yet and the plants are glorious. This time of year is a reminder for me to mark plants I absolutely love. I will also choose what I want for the next year to fill in a few blank spots. I will need to clip some of the grapevine growing around the large window that looks out into my backyard, otherwise I won't be able to see out of it before long. But I love it this way — a little wild. Everything is growing by leaps and bounds. I can hardly wait to see what blooms next.

I am eating spinach, lettuce, radish, and green onions out of the garden. I planted the seeds on St. Patrick's Day, and with a couple coverings on cold nights all the seedlings survived well. It is satisfying and a joy to eat from the tiny seeds that produced these plants in my garden.

I enjoy Mother Earth's garden – the wild and tame plants, the creatures, bees and butterflies. May is a magical month indeed!

SWEET WOODRUFF

Sweet Woodruff has grown in my garden for a long time, and I love greeting it each spring, especially when it blooms little white flowers. This plant is known as the *master of the forest* in Germany. Here in the Midwest it is used as a ground cover in a shady moist area, sometimes under a tree. It likes the east side of my house in an alcove, and since it is most happy there, that is where it will stay.

Sweet Woodruff is a hardy perennial, depending on whether it likes its home or not. It spreads by self-seeding and rhizomes and grows about four inches tall. It does have stringy roots that can choke out other plants, but I have found it lives quite nicely with its neighbors. In my garden it spreads slowly and is easy to pull out to share with friends.

Sweet Woodruff tolerates most soils, and cuttings can be taken in the fall or I dig out clumps of it to share with others. The newly picked leaves and flowers do not really have a fragrance until they have dried, and then they take on the scent of sweet vanilla or honey. I have used the dried leaves in sleep pillows, potpourri and sachets.

In times past, Sweet Woodruff was said to be used to treat kidney and liver, varicose veins, and even heart irregularities, but the leaves do contain tannin, so were used sparingly. It is best known for making the May wine used in the spring ritual of *Beltane*. To make, clip some sprigs and infuse with crushed strawberries in white wine. Let it sit overnight in the refrigerator, strain the next day or evening, and serve in individual glasses or a punch bowl.

It is said that Sweet Woodruff signifies humility as it grows close to the ground like someone who is shy. I love growing Sweet Woodruff and will always grow it in a shady spot in my land-scaping around my home on the preferred east side, and greet it each May with a happy heart.

THE HERB GARDEN

During the late winter months, the herb garden beckoned me like a wayward child wanting its mama. Every time I looked out my window at the wintry dried herb plants, I could feel the tug in my bones to go outside to dig in the dirt and clean out the debris. And with patience, springtime arrived and I could clean, work and dig. I could almost hear my lemon balm, catnip and chives saying, *thank you, thank you, now I can feel the warmth of the sun, and can breathe again.* It felt good welcoming the new little plants once again this spring. I asked my lemon balm plants to please grow quickly as I need to make refreshing tea from their little leaves. Lemon balm is called "the happy plant" for its mood enhancement. It helps to improve mood and is good for the body, mind and soul.

Hope, patience and work –
these are the three graces of spring.
–Ruth Ernest

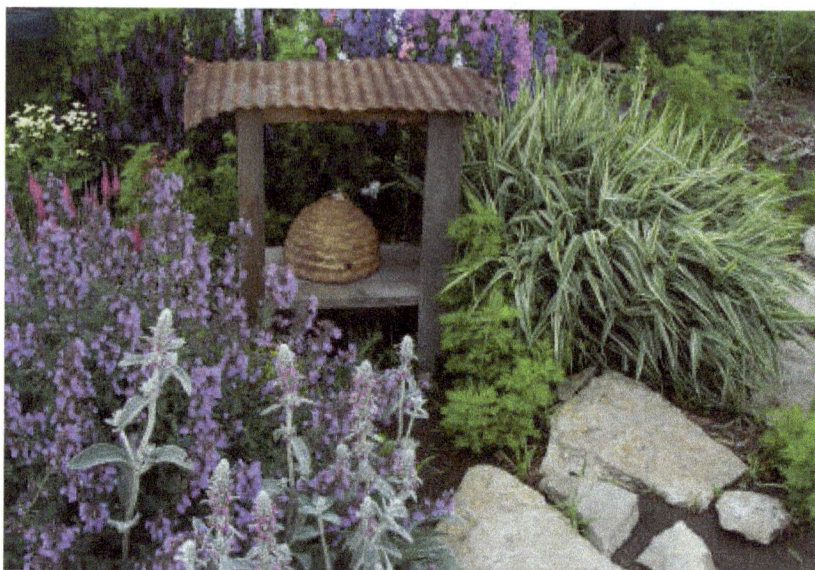

In May, I like to buy a few more herbs to complete what I want and need in my herbal garden, and sometimes I find something that is completely new to me. I watch carefully for the invasive herb plants; some can be controlled and some cannot. I feel all are worth having and working with since I use most of them for food, medicine and tea.

A few invasive herbs are St. Joan's (John's) Wort (the word "wort" means plant/herb), comfrey, nettles, borage, chamomile, mugwort, motherwort and the mint family. Some ivies are considered herbs and will become very aggressive, such as ground ivy (Creeping Charlie). I love the fabulous mints like spearmint, chocolate mint and apple mint, but they send runners underground, creating a mat of roots and take over a garden. I have learned this the hard way, as many gardeners do. I wonder how such a delightful plant could be so overly friendly and not play nice in my garden. The mints need to be planted way out on the "back 40" or in a big half barrel or a big pot. I love spearmint, and use it daily from spring until autumn, keeping the flowering heads clipped off, otherwise the leaves tend to become bitter. The flower heads can also drop seeds, creating new baby plants, but mostly I find it expands through the runners underground. I dry the spearmint for winter use also. Spearmint is the original mint herb. Peppermint is a hybrid from spearmint and a water mint. I find peppermint too strong to use in any of my herbal medicines, as it can sometimes cause reflux, so I find spearmint to be a better choice.

Lemon balm, a member of the mint family, is a favorite of mine. It has behaved quite nicely in my garden so far. Once it begins to flower – and this can happen overnight – I clip it low and a second flush of lemon balm grows. The bees love the mint family, so I leave some lemon balm on the other side of the garage to flower for the bees, and they find it quickly. Lemon balm was originally planted under the hives for the bees. Many herb flowers can be clipped and are delightful used in a tossed green salad or on chicken salad. I also use the flower heads in making vinegar.

Lavender is one of the first plants I plant in an herb garden and one whiff or smell of it will tell you why — it is heavenly. I use the flowers and leaves in potpourri and sleep pillows, as lavender is found to be a great relaxant and anti-depressant. I add a fresh flower stalk of lavender to a cup of hot tea or make cookies from the blossoms. Lavender is quite strong and a little goes a long way. Lavender, as well as Rosemary, sometimes winter over in my Zone 5/6 garden.

Rosemary is used for the brain and to focus. I like to throw a small sprig of rosemary into a hot shower, as the aroma is refreshing, making me more alert and ready to start the day. Foot-long branches of rosemary are good for skewers in the summer when grilling to add flavor, especially the varieties called *BBQ* and *Gorzo*. Remove the leaves first, otherwise this strong scented plant will overpower the flavor of the food. I dry the straight little leaves and use the stem for the skewer. I find having a container planted with rosemary sitting on a porch outside in the summer will not survive the winter, as there is not enough insulation around the pot, so I always plant my rosemary in the earth. And as much as I would love to bring my rosemary and lavender inside for the winter, I find they have a hard time surviving indoors. Here in the Midwest, rosemary is treated as an annual, however with global warming that may change one day. Many varieties of lavender will survive with a little mulching.

National Herb Day and *National Herb Week* is the first week of May each year. I celebrate by planting an herb on May first.

Elizabethan Herb Song

Plant me a garden to heal the body,
Betony, yarrow and daisies to mend
Sage for the blood and comfrey for bones
Foxglove and hyssop the sick to tend
Plant me a garden to heal the heart,
Balm for joy, and the sweet violet
Cowslip, pansies and chamomile
To ease the pain, I want to forget
Plant me a garden to heal the soul,
A garden of peace and tranquility,
Soothed with the scent of lavender
And the heavenly blue of Chicory.

IN THE KITCHEN IN MAY

In May, I pick strawberries to freeze or find them at the grocery store. I begin to think more of the summer season and changing our style of eating from soups and comfort foods to fruits and salads and grilling out.

STRAWBERRY DESSERT
This is a family favorite – it tastes like summer on a cloud
1/2 loaf or cake of angel food cake
1 box (3 oz.) instant vanilla pudding
1 c. cold milk
1 pint (2 c.) vanilla ice cream
1 box (3 oz.) strawberry Jell-O
1 c. boiling water
1 – 10 oz. box frozen sweetened strawberries

Break cake into small pieces; place in 9x9 pan. Dissolve pudding in cold milk and ice cream. Beat until well mixed, pour over cake, do not stir. Let set 30-60 minutes in refrigerator. Dissolve gelatin in boiling water; add strawberries, stir until gelatin begins to thicken, pour over pudding and cake, do not stir. Place in refrigerator until ready to serve. Pieces will not stand alone, but this is more of a thick pudding consistency.

Note: I double for 9x13 pan. I buy a gluten-free angel food cake mix to make and use ¾ of the cake. The recipe overall is easy to make.

I use my own frozen strawberries (2 c. partially thawed and unsweetened) in place of purchased frozen ones.

PLENTIFUL PLANTAIN

Plantain (*Plantago major* and *lanceolota*) is a common weed growing on my land. It grows abundantly and everywhere I look, I see her. *P. Major* is the broadleaf plantain and *P. lanceolota* is the narrowleaf plantain, and both work well in making medicine. In the middle of the summer, plantain sends up her stalk of bloom and the seeds form, which will disperse into the wild, creating more plants another year. The plant itself lies close to the ground with a few leaves upright.

Plantain is the first plant I teach about. She is helpful in healing, and I am grateful she grows on my land as a useful herb. Those who know her remember to put her crushed leaf on a sting or bite, as plantain helps to take the sting, itch or bite away. I am in awe of her capabilities. I collect the plantain leaves in the springtime to dry and make into an oil base for ointment and salve. The fresh leaves can be made into a tincture and used as a spray on bites. But there are other uses for this amazing plant also. It is anti-venom, antibacterial, antimicrobial, antibiotic, anti-inflammatory and has cell-regeneration properties. And there is more – she can clear toxins, deter infection, promote tissue repair and acts as a *drawing agent*. The plant can be used internally and externally. The seeds, which are a cousin to psyllium, are a fiber laxative.

Children love learning about this plant, and I feel it should be the first plant they learn to identify. It has been called *Natures Band-Aid.*

Plantain is useful in mouth issues, as a nourishing diuretic, and is useful in respiratory infections and pneumonia. The leaf is edible raw or cooked but best used when young, as the older leaves become fibrous and tough.

This plentiful plant was also called *White Man's Footprint,* as it likes growing in compacted earth and seemed to appear wherever the new settlers travelled.

When I see a wild herb growing in abundance, I know it is Mother Earth's way of telling me to *take notice* and see how this plant can help me. Plantain gives generously, and I receive and use her gratefully.

Caution: Should not be taken internally during pregnancy and lactation and not used internally in those with intestinal obstruction or hypersensitivity to it.

MAGICAL YARROW

⚜

When I am asked what my favorite herb is, I cannot answer with naming only one. My list of favorite herbs numbers about a dozen. These dozen herbs do what I need them to do, and they cover a large variety of illnesses and healing.

One of the herbs on my list is Wild Yarrow (*Achilliea millefolioum*). She is so important to me that I grow her in a patch close to my house in my flower garden, where she is right at home with her attractive ferny leaves and white umbel flowers. When yarrow begins to bloom, I will ask her to give herself to my medicine making, and then gather the blossoms and leaves from her stalks and use them either fresh or dry for future use in healing oils.

When I moved to my new location in the woods there was mostly shade. There were a couple of sunshine-filled places where I knew a few herbs and flowers would do well. A patch was kept open for the wild white yarrow which I knew needed to be close to me. I started seeds and transplanted to the sunny spot, and since then she has grown well, spreading a little here and there, but can easily be pulled out to share with others. Yarrow is a perennial in my zone 5/6 garden. I find her growing wild in the meadow on the other side of the woods also.

Healing white yarrow is not to be confused with ornamental yarrows which are beautiful but do not have the medicinal qualities of the simple wild yarrow, which is magical and amazing. Yarrow can be used fresh or dried, as a tea, poultice, tincture, oil and vinegar. She is a balancer of fluids in the body and has been called *Master of the Blood*. She is beneficial for kidneys, liver and bladder, with anti-inflammatory and disinfecting properties. Yarrow is also known as *woundwort* because of her ability to stop bleeding, pull wound edges together, ease pain and speed healing. Studies have shown yarrow to be anti-bacterial and effective against strep and staph. Used as a tea, yarrow opens pores, promotes perspiration and breaks fevers. It tastes pungent and bitter as it is an astringent, however I have found when my body is in need of it, the taste comes across as earthy and pleasant. I've used yarrow as a tea for sore throat and congestion. For internal injury or recovery from surgery, I also drink yarrow tea. I have found yarrow tea works well for uterine problems and UTI's (urinary tract infections) when I eliminate sweets. She has been used to help with bruises, incontinence, varicose veins and a myriad of other ailments.

When we teach about yarrow in our *Home Herbalism* course, our students are amazed at what this little plant can do. In an Army study, yarrow tincture was found to outperform Deet, but as with most herbal insect repellents it needs to be applied often – every 45 minutes or so. Yarrow also helps with emotional and mental support by giving us courage to go on in life.

Sweet, little but mighty and magical Yarrow will always live in my garden.

CHILDREN IN NATURE

School will soon be out and children will be home for the summer months. Moms, grandmas and babysitters are wondering how to keep those inquisitive little minds occupied when the kids get bored. I believe summer is an opportunity to teach the children about the earth and Mother Nature and to learn with them.

A perfect solution can be found outside in the Herb Garden. The key is to plan ahead and set a time each day or weekend to be in the garden and outdoors with the children. Several books give good ideas *(listed at end)*.

HERE ARE A FEW THINGS I LIKE TO DO WITH CHILDREN in the herb garden:

— Make lemon balm iced water (instead of sugary lemonade). A lemon balm leaf can be frozen into an ice cube as an added bonus – anything that helps the child to remember and identify this plant another time. I cut six lemon balm stems with leaves about 6 to 8 inches long and one 2- to 3-inch stem of spearmint. I crush the stems in my hands to release the oils/fragrance and put into a quart jar. I have the children do this too and have them smell their hands. I will add enough hot water to fill the jar and put a lid on the hot jar to let it steep and cool down one to four hours. I strain some of the infusion into a glass half full, and fill the rest with cold water. Add some ice. This dilutes it and the children will like its mild lemonade/mint flavor. It does not need a sweetener. I read about lemon balm with the children, teaching about this relaxing and happy herb. Lemon balm water can be frozen in popsicle molds with a few blueberries for interest.

— Make a Nature Bracelet/Armband. Boys and girls alike enjoy doing this. I take a 2-inch wide piece of duct tape and put it "barely snug" (leaving loose enough to cut off later) around the wrist with sticky side facing OUT. Now it is time to start looking for items to stick to the bracelet. The goal is to have the bracelet full of interesting items after our nature walk, and there are always stories to be told as we collect for the bracelet. I pick a small lamb's ear leaf, telling about it as youngsters stick it on the bracelet. Add a lemon balm leaf, a sprig of lavender, perhaps a small daisy flower, a dried berry, a casing from a hatched insect, a bit of moss and so on. Soon the bracelet will be full. *What fun collecting is!*

The bracelet can be carefully cut off when returning to the house or when the child is done collecting, but they may want to wear it all day or all night. To spice it up a little, I like to give the little ones an empty tube from a roll of paper towels. This can be used as a "spy glass" to focus in on those items to add to their bracelets, or to see a bug up close.

— Forage for wild edibles. If the kids like green salads, and many do, I show them the dandelion plant in an unsprayed yard and have them pick a small new leaf to add to their salad (older, larger leaves are bitter) or perhaps a violet flower. I remind them to always check with someone first BEFORE eating anything they pick in the wild. A nature foraging hike is fun, as well as great learning. We take an identification guide along (person or book).

I also have children choose a tree, identify it, talk to it and hug it. We read a poem about a tree. They love making up a story about their particular tree. It is a time for imagination as well as to acquaint the children with Mother Earth and all that grows, and to be outdoors communing in nature. Kids love adventure, hikes in the park or around a lake or wetlands area, and learning what plants and creatures live around them.

I have found it can be a fun summer with children as well as create learning opportunities that will stay with them a lifetime. I call it *Grandma Camp*. Hooray for Summer and Mother Earth!

NATURE BOOKS FOR KIDS

My Nature Journal by Adrienne Olmstead

Walking the World in Wonder, a Children's Herbal by Ellen Evert Hopman

A Kid's Herb Book for Children of All Ages by Lesley Tierra

Wildflower Tea by Ethel Pochocki and Roger Esley (this book has a great story and beautiful illustrations)

COLLECTING BIRD HOUSES

We love the things we love for what they are.
-Robert Frost

I ADMIT IT – I COLLECT *MANY* THINGS! I COLLECT OLD birdhouses in different colors, different shapes, and different sizes. I think I collect birdhouses because they represent *home*. Even a bird needs a home to raise its young. Many birds find their summer home in a hanging basket or bucket, a decorated wreath on a door, or build a nest under the roof of the porch. But others prefer an actual house, perhaps so their nests won't get wet when it rains or blow off a branch when it storms.

EACH YEAR IN THE LATE winter the birdhouses are cleaned out, repaired and readied for a new family of hatchlings. The birdhouses are nailed on fence posts, sit on a bench on the porch, or hang in a tree. I watch the birds collect dried grasses and twigs and take them through the opening in the birdhouse. Some birds make dainty and precise nests while others hastily make their nests out of twigs put this way and that way. By May first, most birds are nesting.

A FEW UNIQUE ANTIQUE AND HANDMADE BIRDHOUSES sit where they can be enjoyed in an old cupboard on the sun porch. They are a joy to see often – some plain and some artistic; all a place to call *home*.

A morning glory at my window satisfies me more than the metaphysics of books.
-Walt Whitman

JENNY WREN

MAKING A HOME

He who shall hurt the little wren
Shall never be beloved by men.
-William Blake

 ren's song is unmistakable and unforgettable.

In reading books about birds, I find much has been written about the wren being an aggressive little bird, and perhaps it deserves every one of those written words. The wren is territorial. But how can such a darling little bird with the operatic trill of an angel have such a bad reputation?

Every spring I eagerly anticipate the arrival of little Jenny wren and her mate. I wait impatiently to hear their song, and when I hear it the world stops for a moment.

They begin singing around Mid-May, close to Mother's Day weekend in my part of the world, and with global warming I would not be surprised this year to hear it a bit earlier.

Once they arrive, the wrens usually nest close to the house, flitting here and there, keeping me company and entertaining me as I work. I open the windows to hear their song. The wrens and I greet the mornings together now in May as I walk through the garden with my hot cup of herb tea in hand. I talk to the wrens, and he sings back a response, completely unafraid, or so it seems. I am excited to have the wrens in my backyard again, as I know they have good appetites for insects of all kinds. And I have to chuckle when busy little Mr. Wren finally entices his lady love Jenny to check out the nesting site he has chosen. He may show her several different sites, with a few twigs in each, and she will take her time checking them all out one by one.

During mating season, the male wren sings his heart out, repeating his song almost a dozen times in a minute as he establishes a territory and finds his mate. The female does not sing often except to reply to her mate. After all there is no time for singing — she has a family to think about. The wrens will have one or two hatchings a year, and when summer is over they normally head to South America for the winter. This last year in Kansas, however, they overwintered here.

One Mother's Day weekend many years ago after we had just moved into a newly built home, my parents visited, bringing with them a little old birdhouse as a housewarming gift (knowing my love for these little houses). The clothesline and posts had just been installed next to my flower garden, and I knew the top of the T-shaped clothesline post would be perfect for a birdhouse. My dad and I attached the birdhouse on one end of the post. Up to this time I had not seen nor heard the wrens yet, but I knew they would soon be back from their winter hiatus. So when the birdhouse was up, I loudly called out, "Mr. and Mrs. Wren, your new home is ready." My dad laughed and said I'd be lucky if I had a sparrow nest in it.

We went back into the house to eat lunch and visit at the big kitchen farm table. The doors and windows were open, as it was a perfect day in May. And lo and behold, within ten minutes of sitting down at the table, a wren was perched on top of the birdhouse we had just put up, singing his heart out. We jumped up from the table and watched that little bird through the big kitchen window for a very long time. My dad was smiling and saying over and over, "I can't believe it. I just can't believe it." It is a memory I will have with me the rest of my life, as my dad has been gone from this earth a long time now. But it happened just like that, and for the next ten years I lived there, I had wrens nesting in that birdhouse every single year. Now when I hear the first wren of May sing his song, I think of my dad.

MEMORIAL DAY

THEY GAVE THEIR ALL

*M*emorial Day was proclaimed in 1868 and was originally called *Decoration Day*. It originated to honor the soldiers who gave their lives for freedom.

The 30th of May was designated for the purpose of decorating the graves of the fallen soldiers who died in defense of our country. Today, the last Monday of May is the time set aside, giving working people a three-day weekend.

I fear sometimes it is forgotten what this designated day is truly all about. Many put flowers on the graves of those ancestors who have walked this earth before us to honor them and for many it is thought of as a weekend for BBQ and camping. I want to remember the fallen soldiers and the ancestors and have BBQ too. Many cemeteries have military celebrations honoring the "gone but not forgotten" soldiers. We cannot forget. After all, there were so many.

> *...These heroes are dead. They died for liberty – they died for*
> *us. They are at rest. They sleep in the land they made free,*
> *under the flag they rendered stainless, and under the solemn*

pines, the sad hemlocks, the tearful willows, and the embracing vines. They sleep beneath the shadows of the clouds, careless alike of sunshine or of storm, each in the windowless Place of Rest. Earth may run red with other wars – they are at peace. In the midst of battle, in the roar of conflict, they found the serenity of death. I have one sentiment for soldiers living and dead: cheers for living, tears for the dead.
-Robert G. Ingersoll

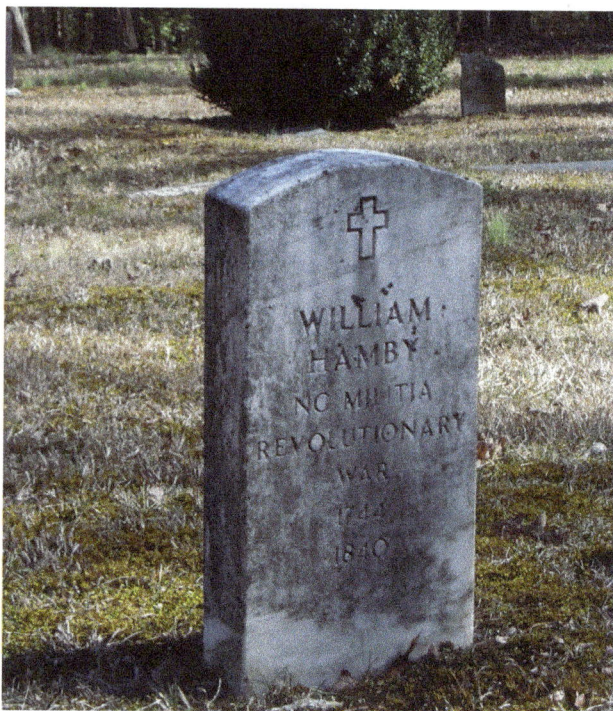

This gravestone marks the grave of a Revolutionary soldier buried in an old small cemetery in Cades Cove National Park in Tennessee. The cemetery was behind an old church and the dates of 1744-1840 were still visible on the marker. We walked the grounds in this beautiful and peaceful hillside cemetery, where the daffodils bloomed along a pathway, leading us into history.

June

THE VIEW FROM MY WINDOW

And what is as rare as a day in June?
Then, if ever, come perfect days.
-James Russell Lowell

S am, my big twenty-five-pound cat, is enjoying a sprig of catnip as I walk through the garden this early morning, greeting everything in sight. Sam prefers to roll in the grass with the catnip in his mouth, ignoring me for the time being.

June has arrived and my focus is on the plants – flowers, herbs, vegetables and of course the weeds!

Lemon balm is calling to me this morning, wishing me a good day. With a smile I ask her if I may clip a few snippets from her large patch to make a healthy herbal cooling drink for later in the afternoon. She nods her OK, and I reach in my pocket for a few strands of my hair, which I removed from my hairbrush this morning, and I lay them at her feet – a gesture of gratitude in exchange for her gift to me. Lemon balm infusion will delight my senses today and help soothe any stress I might encounter.

Lemon balm is a happy perennial plant that is good for the nerves and is the natural, gentle Valium of the herb world. Visitors are surprised when I serve them my infused lemon balm drink. I think they may be expecting lemonade, but lemon balm is mild and even more refreshing. I like to add a touch of fresh spearmint to the infusion to boost the flavor.

Melissa officinalis is commonly called Lemon Balm, and needs to be cut back at the end of June once it begins blooming for a second flush of growth to use for more infusions. I cut sprigs all summer long, using it in my daily infused cool drinks. It is a pretty plant, and I have several large clumps. Lemon balm has very little flavor or fragrance once it is dried, so I mainly use it fresh. I have begun freezing it by making a strong infusion and putting in ice cube trays then double-bagged to use in January; however, its cooling taste is best fresh on a warm summer day.

I believe there are possibilities in the plants we may never know about completely. They have a circulation system, a life force running in their stems as we do through our veins. We already know the plants respond to our touch and our voice, as we do with other people.

Every garden is different in June – some are picture pretty and others wild and tangled, but each feed the gardener's heart and soul, and Mother Nature is my teacher.

> *Almost any garden, if you see it at just the right moment,*
> *Can be confused with paradise.*
> – Henry Mitchell

I remember once again the old adage about plants after they are planted in my garden: *The first year they sleep, the second year they creep, and the third year they leap.* Plants in general thrive while living in community or in close proximity to each other. And after a few years, my plants are intermingling and crossing over each other, enthusiastic and happy growing together.

When the world wearies and society ceases to satisfy,
there is always the garden.
–M. Aumonier

Mother Nature is showing off in June, and the gardens are at their peak, with each day prettier than the last. It is all picture-perfect. My eyes gaze at one plant, then another, and then all together. I want to preserve this scene in my mind and the way it feels forever, but taking a picture does not do it justice. My senses are on overload in June. The fragrance of the Korean lilac, Wentworth viburnum and roses scent the air, as the gentle wind finds us around the corner and a *"come hither and look at me"* beckons me on to another plant and another view of the garden. The colors are vivid after a morning rain shower.

A country garden must have daisies and black-eyed Susans. I gather them often, as they are quite prolific in June. There are many daisies growing and waving in the breeze. They seem to pop up here and there, as well as in my garden, and wherever they bloom they add to the beauty of the landscape. A bouquet of these sweet flowers looks extra special in an old white ironstone pitcher on my wooden kitchen table.

Around the big window in my dining area is an arbor built out two feet on each side and across the top of the window for grapes to grow and twine around. We had a record fourteen inches of rain in May, and the grapes are plentiful on the vine in June. At the base of the arbor I planted a concoction of old-fashioned flowers like columbine, daisies, cleome and zinnias.

The lamb's ear is beautiful. I love it for its leaf color and fuzzy texture in the garden and plant it in spots here and there. It spreads, and soon one little plant can become a big plant. Bees love the blossom stalks. After the stalks have finished blooming I cut the entire plant back to stay attractive the rest of the season with new growth. With the bloom stalks cut back it won't produce seed and babies around the area.

The larkspur is a perennial plant that self-seeds each year, but I find I have a better stand of larkspur if I throw out a few seeds in the very early spring and let them come up where they wish. I love having these beautiful flower stalks blooming in my garden, and they add color to a bouquet for my table.

My garden has a little of *this and that* stuck in *here and there*, like miniature roses, chives to make herbal vinegar, white wild yarrow for the salve I make, and the big Wisteria that covers another huge garden arbor which sometimes blooms and sometimes not. The bittersweet vines blooming along a wood split rail fence will produce bright orange berries in the fall, clematis climbs a trellis, and there is everything in between. My garden is definitely a *wild woman's garden*. It is not orderly – plants touch and caress each other, some are being quite neighborly, and others climb hither and yon.

My garden makes me happy because it is my garden. Everyone needs a garden even if only in a big flowerpot.

It is a perfect morning to grab the umbrella and go to the annual Native Plant Sale in town. So off I go. The parking lot is already full of cars and the sale is just getting ready to open when I arrive. I am happy to see the interest in native plants, re-establishing prairie and woodland habitat, and helping the bees find more good wild food to survive. I knew this would be a good place to find a couple of plants I had been looking for, and I did, but I came home with more. I cannot resist plants needing a good home. When I go to a plant sale or a garden nursery it is like turning a kid loose in a candy store, as my mom used to say. I love the variety of plants. I tend to them like children, watching them grow while telling them how much they are loved, and in return I am given flowers to enjoy. The leaves, roots and flowers will be for medicine making, seedpods for dried gatherings in a vase or wreath, and seeds to pass along to friends.

There is life in the ground where it is stirred up;
it goes into the person who stirs it.
–Unknown

The urge to buy plants in the spring comes naturally when we live close to the earth. This is also an inherited gene, passed down from my mother and grandmothers, and I have passed it along to my daughter who loves the plants also, both tame and wild. The plants I chose to come home with me from the Native Plant sale were wild Beardtongue, wild white Indigo, *Monarda fistulosa* (bee balm) and Liatris. It is thrilling to see native plants growing more abundantly with our help and the offerings of the Native Plant Society. In my state, the roadside ditches are often cleared out by mowing or spraying, much to my dismay. But I'll do what I can on my little piece of land to restore and enjoy these beautiful native plants which are beneficial to insects, birds, and me.

Now the plants from the sale are planted and early evening comes with the sun descending on the western horizon. The moon will be brighter tonight, as the full June moon will appear in all of its glory soon. I'll walk again in the garden and to the edge of the woods, checking everything over one last time today. I am alone, but I feel the grandmothers are with me as I walk tonight. I listen carefully to hear them in the rustling of leaves on the branches of the trees as I say goodnight to all. I watch the sky as another storm is brewing and will bring rain. I feel it in my bones and hear it whispered above me.

That beautiful season, the Summer!
Filled was the air with a dreamy and magical light;
And the landscape lay as if newly created
in all the freshness of childhood.
-Henry Wadsworth Longfellow

THE FULL MOON IN JUNE

June, O moon of Summer,
Shine to leaves of grass, catalpa,
and all silver under your rain tonight.
-Carl Sandburg, 1878-1967

Strawberry moon is one of the names given to the June full moon. The wild strawberries ripen in the month of June, and what a delicious find these berries would have been for the early Native Americans and settlers. I look for the wild strawberries today in my meadow.

The full moon of June was called several names to identify this time of year. It was called the *Rose Moon* as the wild prairie roses come into bloom in June. It was also known as the *Honey Full Moon* as the bees are busy making honey. And another name for the June full moon was *Full Flower Moon*. Some tribes called it the *Milk Full*

Moon, the *Mother Moon* or the *Corn Planting Full Moon*. It was a time of increased fertility, and many plants bloom in the month of June.

Since I was a young adult I have been intrigued by the names of the full moons and how the ones who walked before us used the moon as a timetable to gauge what was happening in nature and on the land.

In June, my *Moon Tea* blend is lemon balm, spearmint, a sprig or two of lavender and a few rose petals – these are happy, calming and relaxing herbs. It is a delightful time to make *Moon Tea* with children or grandchildren and teach them about the earth and the moon, the names for the moon this month, and how the moon pulls the tides of the ocean. It is a time to dance in the moonlight or just be still and listen to the sounds of nature around us when the moon shines bright.

> *See how nature – the trees, flowers,*
> *grass grows in silence;*
> *See the stars, the moon, and the sun,*
> *how they move in silence....*
> *We need silence to be able to touch souls.*
> -Mother Teresa

IN THE GARDEN IN JUNE

A garden of herbs is a garden of things loved for themselves in their wholeness and integrity. It is not a garden of flowers, but a garden of plants which are sometimes very lovely flowers
– and are always more than lovely flowers.
-Henry Beston, *Herbs and the Earth*

The enjoyable work in my herb garden begins early in the season. When I harvest will depend on whether we have an early or late spring, and a mild or tough winter. With the arrival of June first I have a lot of harvesting started, but there is still much to do in the month of June.

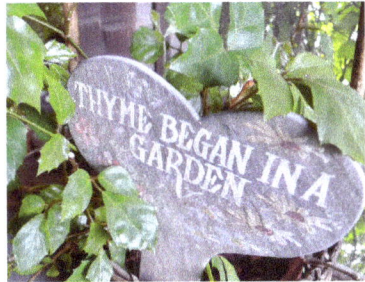

Once the herbs begin flowering, the energy goes into the flowers and setting the seed; to reproduce is the job of the plant. The leaves become a bit tougher and sometimes a little bitter once the plant flowers. I used to think that if we keep the flowers pinched off, the leaves would stay tender and tasty, and this is true up to a point. Year after year, I have tried it various ways, but I cannot change Mother Nature. I clip off the flowers of basil, putting them into white wine vinegar to make delicious herbal vinegar to use and give as gifts. But the plants are set on one purpose in June, and that is flowering, setting seed, and reproducing. When I know this is going to happen, it is time to prepare and begin gathering the flowers and leaves. The flowers are not only beautiful and fragrant, but also tasty and beneficial to us. I always grow a plant or two for me and one or more to flower for the bees.

The chives were beautiful this early spring, as they always are, with their violet colored flower-ball heads. But there is only about a week's window to gather them, and this is true of many plants. It is important they be collected at their peak. And then I have a difficult decision to make: to leave them alone, looking pretty in the garden for the time being or clipping their blooms while vibrant and making the vinegar I love to use in the kitchen. In the end, I will gather some and leave some. The flowers I leave in the garden to bloom will be pretty a little while longer and then they start to fade, and as they near the end of their cycle and are making lots of seeds in the heads, I gently clip them and dry the seeds to give to others.

With all herbs I cut and bring into the house to dry, I use the same method – laying them on the center island on a clean big white dishtowel. I keep a small fan on the herbs at a distance to stir the air gently and dry them more quickly, especially on humid days. I keep the herbs whole and do not crumble or compact them as I place them into a jar to store them. Keeping the herbs as whole as possible means they will stay vibrant longer. I put a folded plain paper towel in the bottom of the jar in case there might be a bit of moisture left. Then I fill the jar, label it and set in a dark cupboard. I also hang herbs to dry, but I have found they are more likely to mold, and it can be hard to remove the leaves once dry. For dried herbs, the key for preservation is making sure they are completely dried before storing.

HERE IS MY METHOD FOR MAKING HERB VINEGAR: I DO not wash my herbs. I wait at least two to three days after a rain or watering my garden before I pick (when my herbs are about ready I watch the weather forecast intently). By not washing and waiting at least two days after a rain or watering, the fragrant oils and good constituents are fully present, not washed out or washed away. It also reduces the water content in the plant. Too much water content in the plant can dilute the vinegar and may spoil the batch. I cut my herbs, bring them into the house, and lay them out on a table or kitchen island on the one-yard square white cotton dishtowel. I let the plants rest on the towel for an hour or so, giving time for the little critters that are residing in the flower heads a chance to escape, and I help by tapping the herbs on the towel to dislodge them. The insects are easy to see on a white cotton towel.

I use a recycled glass bottle and stuff in sprigs of fresh herbs and fill the bottle to cover the herbs with white *wine* vinegar. Herb vinegars can be made to taste. I often add other herbs to enhance or boost flavor. The herb vinegar becomes somewhat stronger the longer it sits. The vinegar needs to sit two moons (at least six weeks) in a dark cupboard before using. If giving the herb vinegar as a gift, I strain the herbs out and add a few fresh herbs to make it attractive.

I never set an infusion or my vinegar in the sun. As pretty as it may look, the vinegar will be better set on a dark shelf. Vinegars can be made from lavender, basil, lemon herbs, chives, dandelion flowers, rose petals, dill and other edible flowers and leaves.

The fragrant vinegar makes a wonderful addition to salad dressing when added to olive oil, salt and pepper with a little honey. I sprinkle the herb vinegar over roasted veggies when removing from the oven, use as a marinade for meat or sprinkle over meat before roasting; I add to deviled eggs and potato salad, chicken salad and more.

Here are a few things I am doing in my herb garden in June:

- Collecting rose petals. I use them fresh for making jelly and dry the petals for making potpourri. I also add fresh or dried rose petals to my infusion to drink throughout the year.

- Clipping Queen Anne's lace to press and dry the pretty flowers for note cards. I will make jelly from Queen Anne's lace the same day it is picked, beginning with an infusion for the liquid in the recipe. **Always** be sure to positively identify Queen Anne's lace (or any wild herb) before using, as there are poisonous look-alikes.

- Clipping spearmint to dry for winter and leaving some fresh in the garden for summer beverages.

- Giving a sprig of catnip to Sam, my big orange tabby cat.

- Watching the elderberries bloom and set fruit.

- Making homemade insect repellent.

- Cutting the lavender when it is budded but not yet blooming to make lavender wands or small bouquets for gift giving.

- Picking and drying plantain and other herbs for making salve.

- Observing nature and being mindful of all things around me.

- Being grateful for my gardens that provide me with food for body and soul, fragrance for the senses and a bit of enchantment along the way.

IN THE KITCHEN IN JUNE

CHICKEN SALAD

3 c. finely chopped cooked chicken
2 stalks celery, finely diced
1/2 c. toasted pecans, coarsely chopped
1 c. red seedless grapes, quartered or halved
1 tbsp. fresh tarragon or thyme, finely chopped
1/4 c. red onion, finely chopped
3/4 c. mayonnaise
1 tsp. Dijon mustard
Salt & Pepper to taste

Mix, taste, season and adjust according to taste. Serve on open face bun or leaf lettuce.
Optional: Add a few fresh edible flowers to top before serving.

BLT SALAD

5-6 c. lettuce, torn into pieces
1 lb. cooked elbow or shell macaroni

1 lb. cooked bacon, crumbled (not bacon bits)
4 large tomatoes, cut in smaller pieces
3 boiled eggs, chopped
3 green onions, sliced

Toss all together
Note: add dressing an hour before serving

Dressing:
3/4 c. mayonnaise or salad dressing
1 T. red wine vinegar
1/2 tsp. salt
1/2 tsp. sugar
Whisk dressing and toss salad a half hour before serving.

SUMMER SOLSTICE

The Summer Solstice occurs after mid-month in June. It ushers in summer and is the longest day and shortest night of the year. Sol-stice means sun-still. The day lengthens and the sun rises higher until it seems to stand still in the sky on this day. Earth has now reached the midpoint of her journey around the sun and our daylight hours will begin to shorten again.

John Burt writes about the Solstice saying, "The sun's energy, absorbed by the plants, fuels all life on earth. The summer solstice brings hours of sunlight and the most luxuriant plant growth. Morning sunlight is used to create a flower essence: the sun's rays convey a plant's unique vibrational life force into patterns, beliefs, and emotions, freeing us to connect again with oneness. A balanced and peaceful mind intuitively aligns with healthy choices for all. Plant wisdom holds information and support of holistic living and healing, recalling time when man lived in balance with nature's harmony."

LAVENDER

⚒

The air was fragrant with a thousand trodden aromatic herbs,
with fields of lavender and with the brightest roses
blushing in tufts all over the meadows ....
-William Cullen Bryant

*H*ow can anyone resist the fragrance of lavender? Like
roses, this is an irresistible herb. I like growing it and
using it and am happy just being near where it is growing. For the
bees and me, I grow no less than three lavender plants. It is a
powerful plant in many ways.

IN MY AREA OF THE MIDWEST, THE VARIETIES
recommended for hardiness are *Hidcote, Grosso* and *Munstead*.
Usually my lavender will overwinter, but not if there are many
bitterly cold days in succession. This last year, after a wonderful
autumn, we had eleven consecutive days when the weather was
bitter cold with nighttime temps close to zero in December. The
talk amongst the gardeners was that we would lose some plants,
and we did. The rosemary and lavender surrendered to winter.

Then there are winters, several in a row, where the lavender survives beautifully. I am determined now to watch the weather forecast more closely and have protection ready for the lavender in the bitter cold of winter.

I make lavender sugar, lavender cookies, dream pillows and a lavender sniffing jar for my emotional well-being. I love lavender made into fragrant wands for putting in a lingerie drawer or giving as a gift.

TO DRY LAVENDER, I PICK THE FLOWER STEM AT THE beginning of its bloom cycle while still in the bud stage. If lavender is picked in full bloom, it will drop its flowers when dry. I like to hang lavender in small bunches in my home. If I trim the plant back, the needle-like leaves can be used in potpourri or dream pillows, as the stems and needle leaves are fragrant also.

According to the American Botanical Council (ABC) in Germany, lavender is licensed as a standard medicinal tea for sleep disorders and nervous stomach. I add a sprig or two to the half-gallon or gallon jar of moon tea I make when lavender is in full bloom.

Many find lavender hard to grow, and in clay soil it is a problem, but I have found digging the hole deeper and adding gravel for drainage at the bottom does help. Lavender does not like wet feet. It can be "hilled" or planted at the top of a mound. It likes alkaline soil, so adding a little lime helps, as well as bone meal. Lavender likes full sun, and fares much better when it is planted close to the house on the south side.

Lavender has many uses and is always welcomed in my garden.

LAVENDER COOKIES

1 stick butter
1 c. sugar
2 eggs
1 ½ c. plus 1 T. flour
2 tsp. baking powder
Dash salt
1 tsp. dried lavender buds (chopped or muddled in mortar and pestle)
½ tsp. vanilla

Mix butter and sugar. Add eggs and beat well. Add dried ingredients and mix. Cover with plastic wrap and refrigerate overnight (or at least 4 hours). Next day prepare cookie sheet with parchment paper. Make dough into 1-inch or slightly larger balls. Roll in sugar. Bake at 350 for 12-15 minutes, taking out before edges brown. Let cool on cookie sheet before removing. I bake only one cookie sheet at a time in oven (not 2) as they bake more evenly if heat is allowed to distribute around.

ROSES

One comes back to these old-fashioned roses as one does to music and old poetry. A garden needs old associations, old fragrances, as a home needs things that have been lived with.
-Marian Pagge

June is the most popular month for weddings and the common flower for brides to carry is the rose. The rose is the queen of the flowers and can be found in most gardens in one form or another.

The roses in my garden and on my arbor are in full bloom now. The fragrance is heady, and I pick a large open flower to float in a clear bowl of water on the table as an elegant centerpiece.

The Rose was designated as the *Herb of the Year* in 2012 by the *International Herb Society*. The rose is also an herb, which means it is a useful plant and can be used medicinally, in cooking and in crafting.

Medicinally, we think of the rose hips as being full of Vitamin C and useful when one has the common cold. Rose hip oil is used in anti-aging serum. Pure rose essential oil is very expensive to buy, as it takes a truckload of rose petals to make a small vial of this fragrant oil.

Today there are many varieties of roses, and if I ask anyone to name their favorite rose I will get a different answer from each person. Most modern day roses are beautiful to look at but are not always fragrant. I prefer the old-fashioned rose, which is more of an apothecary rose, with a pretty flower and full of fragrance. There are hybrids, teas, floribundas, shrub, miniatures and climbers to choose from. The one thing I have learned through gardening experience is this: if I choose a climber I need to remember that it *really* does climb and it will be in that spot forever. My advice is to choose a rose wisely, and more importantly choose carefully where it is to be planted. Climbing roses are beautiful and have been known to live hundreds of years. The climbing rose is the one rose you can still find growing around very early abandoned homesteads, sometimes growing up the windmill, which gives it good support. The climbing rose seems to want to reach the heavens above.

I am partial to the miniature roses now. They take up little space, have abundant blooms and come in beautiful colors. I have found them to be quite hardy here in the Midwest. Big chain grocery stores sometimes carry them in their floral department for a reasonable price. The miniatures grow well in my Midwest garden, and I now have no less than five of various colors in my garden. A favorite mini rose is a pale pink one I ordered from a garden company called *Belinda*. It grows about 2.5-foot tall, but my other miniature rose bushes are shorter.

Roses should be collected when newly open, as the older blooms lose much of their color and fragrance when dried. I collect before the heat of the day, usually mid-morning or close to noon. The volatile oils have increased in the rose by this time and the dew of the night has evaporated. I do not rinse the petals as they are too delicate, and Mother Nature has already done that with the dew from the night. My roses are not sprayed or dusted, so they can be used for food and beverages. It is important to never use florist or grocery store flowers for food or medicine, as they have been treated with chemicals to extend their blooms.

Rose jelly is a delicacy I have made several times. To make, I infuse the petals in hot water like a tea, let cool, strain, measure and use in a basic jelly recipe that uses a little apple juice.

Rose petals can be used fresh in a salad. I like to remove the lower white thumbnail portion of the petal by nipping it off, as it can be bitter tasting.

Full Moon Tea (infusion) is made with fresh lemon balm leaves and stems and rose petals for a delightful beverage. *Full Moon Tea* can be made the night before and the night after a full moon as well as the night of the full moon. The rays from the full moon add energy, so I sit the jar out in an open area on the earth. The next morning, I strain and refrigerate it, drinking it during the day as-is or over ice.

To make a half-gallon jar of infusion, I add a couple handfuls of lemon balm, twisted or chopped up, the petals of one small rose and sprig or two of blooming lavender flower stalks or a sprig of mint. This is a favorite potion of mine and also for guests that happen by. A tiny rosebud or petal can be frozen in ice cubes and is impressive when serving to guests.

Rose syrup is made by layering pure cane sugar with rose petals in a pint jar. Leave it sit a few days on the counter as everything dissolves, and soon it becomes fragrant, delicious rose syrup. Strain and refrigerate. It will be strong, so use sparingly. I have used in frostings for cakes, drizzled over strawberries and blueberries, or anything I dream up.

Crafters have hung roses to dry for use in potpourri mixes for years. Another method is to gather the roses and scatter the petals on a white cotton dishtowel to dry for several days. The house will smell heavenly as the petals dry in the open air. The dried rose petals can be used in potpourri or put in a fragrance jar mixed with a little lavender and a few cloves. This combination is wonderful together for calm and relaxation and nice for gift-giving. Dried petals are good to add to a tea blend in the winter to uplift one's spirit or for those who are depressed or grieving. Fragrant roses have a strong rosy taste and can overpower in a tea or drink (as lavender will as well), so use sparingly.

Everything is coming up roses in my little corner of the world!

ANTIQUES AS GARDENING DÉCOR

or a while I lived in the mountains of Colorado, where the cool air and short season hindered having a garden. The high altitude made it almost impossible. When I moved back to Nebraska on seventeen acres, I was anxious to start gardening once again. How does one begin where there was once only prairie? Selecting an area for a vegetable garden and another area for herbs and flowers was the first step. I learned not only about gardening and plants, but also how to create a garden that would feed my spirit.

With the wild nothingness of wide-open spaces, contemplating a garden can be overwhelming. I have found creating perimeters and borders to delineate spaces makes the vastness seem more manageable.

At first, I sat an old chair in the middle of the space I thought would work, and then visualized the meandering paths and what plants would go where. A chair is a necessity in a garden – not only to rest but to dream.

Behind the house we installed a new picket fence to designate a large area for an old-fashioned flower and herb garden. The new fence soon weathered into a soft old gray. At the entrance of the garden, a large rustic arbor was built of treated lumber, and the top was covered with large branches to give the space an old and welcoming natural look. American wisteria, a climbing pink rose and clematis were planted to climb to the top and over. In the middle of the fenced area, we placed an eight-foot tall obelisk made from large twigs and branches, and then we anchored it well so it would not blow over with the never-ending prairie winds. The obelisk was topped with a birdhouse and around the base I planted herbs. Paths were added, going in each of the four directions from the obelisk, sectioning off the large area for individual flower and herb beds. We planted several crab apple trees on the outer edges to give color, height and structure.

HAVING BEEN IN THE ANTIQUES BUSINESS FOR MANY years, I look at most items as having a second life or another use in today's world. Here are a few ideas I have used in my various gardens to add texture, interest and structure:

- Old metal gates are used in my gardens, one as an actual gate to enter the garden, and the other one staked down with flowers planted around and a wreath hung on the gate.

- Old cement birdbaths, now cracked, can be planted with creeping thyme or a low flowerpot filled with trailing flowers set inside.

- An old wheelbarrow can be used to hold containers of flowers and decorated seasonally.

- I place an old unusable wooden bench in the garden and set a birdhouse or an old metal watering can on it for interest.

- Old iron machinery wheels are decorative along a fence and vines will grow well on the spokes.

- An old wooden ladder, cut down to size and anchored to the ground or a wall makes a quick upright trellis.

- A old bicycle with faded paint perched in the garden becomes a focal point when pots of flowers are placed in its wire basket. I like ornamental sweet potato vines trailing down with purple and bright green leaves.

- An old metal wash boiler, once used to boil water to wash clothes, makes a good planter.

- Large old galvanized tubs, used long ago as bathtubs, can become a wonderful container garden planted with ornamental cabbage, flowers or herbs. Add a couple of old hand garden tools stuck in the soil and a garden sign with a neat saying on it. I have even made a fairy garden in an old washtub. (Be sure this tub is planted where you want it to stay as it becomes very heavy once filled with earth).

- An old iron baby bed or full-sized iron bed can be painted or left to rust. When planted with flowers in the open part, it literally becomes a "flower bed."

- Broken terra cotta flowerpots make natural looking signs to identify plants and herbs. Save the larger shards of the broken pots and use a permanent marker to write the name of the plant on the clay piece and stick in the ground beside the plant to identify it.

OTHER UNUSUAL OLD PIECES CAN BE USED IN CREATIVE ways. An old walking plow is one of the pieces I have enjoyed in my side yard over the years. It sits in front of a cluster of three Viburnum shrubs, adding nostalgia with its history, and is a centerpiece for a section of the otherwise bare yard. The walking plow was the original garden tiller.

Lastly, I make sure I have a neat old chair, as every avid gardener needs to rest once in awhile. Adding a few old-fashioned flowers in the garden like zinnias, hollyhock, and larkspur will make the antiques feel right at home.

To maximize the use of unique old pieces in the garden, I use a decorating technique also used in my home, called *layering*.

Layering adds interest as well as depth. For example, I wanted to hide the air conditioning unit next to the house, so we installed a section of tall wood fence a couple feet in front of it (still allowing for good air circulation so it would work well). On the solid wood fence section, I hung an old, many-paned glass window frame with the glass removed and with old chipped white paint still adhered to it. This created interest to the wood fence section. Colorful hollyhocks grow on each side of the fence, and an old park bench sits in front of it all, inviting one to sit awhile.

I take pictures when I think the vignette is complete, as a picture tells the story. By looking at the photograph, it gives me perspective on whether the decorating is too much, not enough or just right. It is always easy to add another container of plants or take one away.

Vines are an easy way to create layers and to conceal architectural elements that we deem unsightly. I use Virginia creeper and Boston ivy vines to cover the cement side walls of my walkout basement. The vines soften the look of hard concrete. These two types of vines grow fast and turn a brilliant orange-red in the fall. Silver lace vine grows quickly also and will cover swings, arbors and fences. The side of my screened-in porch is shaded nicely in the summer by a lush silver lace vine entwined on an attached wide trellis. More vigorous vines such as bittersweet, honeysuckle, trumpet vine and wisteria are better for using further from the house covering substantial fences and arbors. I love the American wisteria and bittersweet available at garden centers. The trumpet vine I would not use again as it is very invasive.

I plant vines, create a few borders, add antique and unusual pieces to create interesting layers, toss in some heirloom flower seeds, and my garden is a delight for me and everyone who visits.

July

THE VIEW FROM MY WINDOW

Look out into the July night,
and see the broad belt of silver flame
from which flashes up the half of heaven,
fresh and delicate as the bonfires of the meadow-flies.
-Ralph Waldo Emerson

*W*elcome Sweet July!

Childhood memories seem to resonate mostly in July for me. July was picking fresh fruit, family reunions and picnics, climbing trees, fireworks and silvery sparklers, eating watermelon and letting the juice run down our chins, searching for blinking lightning bugs, drinking lemonade and everything in-between. *Oh, the joys of summer!*

And now that I am older, more words enter my vocabulary when I want to describe the month of July. Words like: hot, sweltering heat, humidity, summer storms, children out of school, eating fresh produce from my garden, a gentle breeze on a very hot day, and escaping to the air conditioning of my home when the stifling heat becomes too much to handle.

Living today in this moment, I am mindful of all the yesterdays. I pull all of the July memories together and then add new descriptions as I go along. I love living month-to-month with the seasons. I am conscious of being mindful while celebrating and enjoying the simple pleasures of each month, not letting the days slip by too quickly without savoring each and every one. It is a way I have come to appreciate each day of each month – the seasons of nature and of my life. Without doing this intentionally, the time is gone without interacting with the months and the seasons. The interacting is what creates memories.

Today it will be stormy. I like rainy days, especially in July, when the sun-baked earth needs to cool down and the drink from the sky revives it again. It will turn hot and muggy as the day progresses and is typical of a summer day in July in the Midwest. Even then there are moments to appreciate, like a tall cool glass of iced herb tea.

Early on this late July day, before the storms think of beginning, I collect fresh produce from the garden. In my gathering basket I add zucchini, banana peppers, green beans, garlic and tomatoes, and this will become the fixings for the main meal today. I will make a stir-fry of veggies and add a baked chicken breast. When ready to serve I will add chopped basil leaves, a dash of stir-fry sauce and freshly grated Parmesan cheese. This is a meal fit for royalty. Growing my own organic vegetables doubles the enjoyment, but if I were unable to grow my own I would buy organic at the Farmers Market each week, supporting my local growers.

July and fireworks are synonymous. I loved fireworks as a kid. Being poor and living in the country, my parents did not buy fire-works except a few sparklers, so we would drive into town seven miles away, and there we would sit on a blanket on the park grounds and watch the colors light up the sky. Now that I am older, I have a different opinion of fireworks. A little is okay, and I know big fireworks displays have become traditional in many big cities. I think the towns could spend their money more wisely. It seems wasteful when it could be given to a charity for a better purpose. Now and then I have to climb up on my "soap box." The money spent on fireworks is gone forever and really not helped anyone. Perhaps I have become disenchanted as I age, but I don't think so, as I am enchanted by so much in life. It all comes down to choices we make. The loud noises scare small children and frighten animals. I much prefer nature's "thunder-boomers" than manmade ones. It was after 11 p.m. when the countryside finally quieted down this year after the fireworks celebrations. I stepped outside my front door and the smell of sulfur from the fireworks lingered in the evening breeze – it was not the sweet smell of nature and the woods around me. But then again, July 4th comes only once a year.

On this early July 4th night as I peer into the darkened trees in the woods, I see the flickering of nature's fireworks – the fireflies winking and blinking in the air. As a child we called them lightning bugs and would watch impatiently at night to see who could spot the first flicker of the bugs in the air, and then we would try to catch them, running and tripping over rocks as we would peer into the darkness to see a little flying blinking bug. Sometimes we would catch them and sometimes not. It was a rite of passage of my childhood, as well as for my children and grandchildren. As a child we would take off the part of the bug that lit up and stick it on our ring finger and call it our "diamond ring" and it would sparkle in the night! And I don't think then we ever gave a thought to that poor bug – I shudder when I think about harming them now.

As a young mother, I helped my children collect a few fireflies to put in a jar. We would screw a lid on tightly and lay it beside their pillow at night to become their friendly bug nightlight. I would tell my children while they were sleeping in the night the fireflies would fly back to their families. When they fell asleep, I would take the jar outside and let the fireflies go back into the wild. The next morning it was never questioned, and I just smiled to myself. Everyone was content. The children fell asleep happily, the fireflies were back in nature, and all was right in our world.

If you catch a firefly and keep it in a jar
You may find that you have lost a tiny star.
If you let it go then back into the night,
You may see it once again – star bright.
-Lillian Moore

The lightning bug or firefly is part of nature's nightlife and is neither a bug nor a fly – it is a beetle. Today I wish I could find a few to catch again and savor their sparkle in a jar, but there do not seem to be nearly as many as there were when my children were small. Will this little beetle become an endangered species one day in my wooded backyard like the butterflies and bees have become? I am saddened by this thought. I plant a habitat for insects and do not use pesticides nor herbicides on my acreage, wishing everyone would help protect nature's miracles. I wonder to myself if my great-grandchildren will ever experience a butterfly flitting around the flowers during the day or a firefly showing its blinking light in the night?

It is mid-July now, and last night the Super Moon graced our summer sky. News reports are saying it was larger and brighter than our normal full moon. I pulled my outdoor chair to a clearing to view this nighttime treasure. I talked to the big moon and then sang to her. I started to compose a poem in my head about the moon which began with, *Hello Moon, your light is so bright, listen to my thoughts tonight.* I love seeing the super moons, the blue moons and the harvest moons and ALL the full moons.

It is the season of summer when July appears on the calendar. I find working outside between 7 and 9 a.m. are best when it is a bit cooler and the sun does not burn as quickly, but the humidity is still present on this July early morning, and soon I am wiping the sweat from my brow. The mosquitoes bite more in the early morning hours, so it becomes a toss-up between being bitten by mosquitoes or the hot sun beating down on me. I choose the early morning hours, as I have more energy then too. I apply homemade mosquito repellent liberally to keep those dratted *skeeters* away. As I am weeding out the foxtail, watering the thirsty plants and swatting a mosquito away, I also think about the beauty and joys to be found in the month of July.

Summer is the season I was longing for last February! In July, I don't have to wear many clothes on the hottest of days, and I don't. Many days a tank top and cut off old jeans are my attire – not a pretty sight I am sure – but the birds and other wildlife never complain. Back in these woods if anyone needs to stop by they will call first (a neighborly thing to do), so I don't worry about the "proper" gardening attire – whatever that means. I dress for comfort in the summertime.

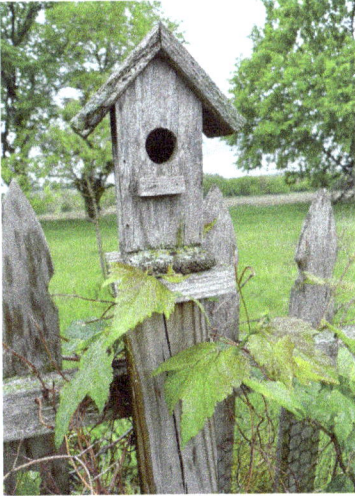

Watching the birds come to the birdbath is a summer joy. The birdbaths are kept clean and I fill them with fresh water each morning on these hot days. The birds enjoy a drink now and then and sometimes a leisurely bath. I have two large birdbaths on pedestals plus small ones on the ground. One birdbath is made from quick-setting concrete I formed around a big rhubarb leaf and another around a large hosta leaf. These birdbaths sit on the ground in the flower beds where the birds, skinks (little black lizards that live here), frogs, squirrels and other small animals can find a quick sip of refreshing water on a hot day.

The lemon balm has been cut back for a second flush of new growth, making it usable once again for my summertime iced drink. And once the other herbs flower, as most have by July, they are not that good to use anymore, as the leaves turn bitter when they are in their reproductive cycle. I cut some of the herb flowers to dry and use in wreaths and bouquets later, but I always leave a few for visiting bees and butterflies to enjoy.

By the end of July, the elderberry's plump heavy heads are drooping and need gathering. At times, I clip the heads and take the berries off with the tines of a fork, pulling it through the stems, nudging the berries to fall into a waiting bowl or use the whole heads in a pan. August is busy, so I may clip the berry heads short and freeze the whole heads until January when the pace slows and I have time to work with them. If I am low on elderberry tonic, then I must make time to do up a batch to help fight off colds and flu. I also make elderberry jelly this time of year for my grandsons as a special treat from Grandma and Mother Earth.

When I go into the backyard garden or take a walk down my long country lane to go to the mailbox, I always find a few things to put into my pocket. I carry a small bag or basket with me most times when I am out, and I gather – yes, I am a *gatherer*. The "treasures" I find and gather depend on the time of year. The usual bounty I find to put in my basket may be herbs to dry or to use fresh, wild-flowers for a vase on my table, or a leaf of a wild plant to identify later. Other items finding their way into my basket this time of year might be berries, seed pods, a pinecone, feather, a lichen-covered piece of branch, a small rock shaped like a heart, or a little wildflower in bloom to press in an old book. I find all these items absolutely irresistible. I will use some of the items; others will be put into an antique wooden bowl to look at often as reminders of time spent in Nature. Even in the heat of a July day I find wonderful treasures, and in looking for them I become more aware and mindful of what is around me and the little details of Nature.

It is the sweet, simple things of life
which are the real ones after all.
-Laura Ingalls Wilder

A few things on my July agenda are:

— Re-vamping the fairy garden I made in May to make it through until autumn.

— Sitting on the porch right after sundown and watching for fireflies to dance as the sky darkens into nighttime.

— Putting away the Queen Anne's lace jelly I made, which is a favorite of grandson Dylan. A few flowers and leaves of Queen Anne's lace still need to be collected, pressed and dried to use on note cards later.

— Collecting tansy leaves that look like beautiful ferns to press and dry to use in collages.

— Clipping thyme, rosemary, dill and chives to chop finely and use in potato salad for a family supper.

— Continuing to pick green beans.

— Cutting Rosemary stalks to use as kabob skewers on the grill – they impart a wonderful flavor.

— Picking yellow pear tomatoes, which are producing a couple handfuls a day – but only a handful comes into the house with me, as I snack on the others right off the vine. Tomatoes in July right off the vine – what's not to love?

— Picking more oregano flowering stems. The pretty purple, lavender, and pink blossomed stems are laid in an old flat-bottomed flower gathering basket. Bees are busily buzzing telling me they are enjoying the flowers too (and this year I have a few more bees as the neighbors have put in a hive). The big stand of oregano self-seeds and sends out underground runners, so I have more than I need. And as I walk into the house with my flowering oregano stalks, a honeybee follows me in as if she wants to say *thank you* for planting the flowers so she and her friends could enjoy them too. The best quality of herbs will always be the ones I collect and dry myself.

— Taking pleasure in the blessed bounty of wild and tame herbs and filling my cupboard shelves with tinctures and infusions for medicines, and drying bunches of herbs to hang from nooks and crannies to be used in salves, food, and wreaths.

ON MY WALKS, I HAVE NOTICED THE DITCHES AND meadows are extra abundant this summer with elderberry, milkweed, Monarda, black-eyed Susans and Queen Anne's lace. The abundance of elderberry has me wondering in the back of my mind if this a sign of a hard winter to come. Folklore says that abundant harvest is Mother Nature preparing the creatures of the earth, including me, to survive a harsh winter ahead. I will make a note of this in my journal and see what the winter brings.

Although it is hot and humid in July, I find there are many joys and blessings in the middle of the year. I pour a glass of lemon balm and spearmint infused tea over ice on this 100-degree July day and sit on my front porch viewing my world around me. It is time to relax and do nothing but daydream.

Rest is not idleness, and to be sometimes on the grass
on a summer's day listening to the murmur of the water,
or watching the clouds float across the sky,
is by no means a waste of time.
- John Lubbock

THE FULL MOON IN JULY

Nature is not a place to visit – it is home.
-Gary Snyder

There are many names for the July summertime full moon. Native Americans and early settlers named the season in which they were living one full moon to the next full moon. When I study the names for the full moon, I smile and I think back to that long-ago time when the people of this land lived before there were clocks or calendars.

Thunder moon and *Full Moon of Storms* were names used because of the fierce summer storms of July that came up suddenly and frequently. I have to believe that these summer storms frightened the people living back then, not knowing what would happen next. Our weather forecasts today forewarn us, and our calendars tell us which month of the year it is.

Full Hay Moon was named as the mowing of hay began in the month of July.

Full Buck Moon meant the deer and elk bucks begin to grow new antlers at this time of year. *Buffalo Mating Moon* also occurred in July.

I gaze at the full moon in wonderment, knowing it is part of me. I work with the full moon to decant my tinctures and to make full moon tea under the energy rays of the moon.

> *Moon, sister Moon, shining so high —*
> *Smile down upon me, Full face in the sky*
> *Moon, sister Moon, with your silver glow*
> *Whisper your secrets –*
> *tell me what you know.*
> -*Moving Breath* from Album, "She Changes"

IN THE GARDEN IN JULY

Go out, go out I beg of you
And taste the beauty of the wild.
Behold the miracle of the earth
With all the wonder of a child.
-Edna Jacques

The weeds have taken over my garden. It is July and foxtail season. As soon as I think the garden is looking good and the mulch is down, more foxtail appears. It is relentless.

The garden soil is amended each year, and the seeds blow in on the winds. Weeds love to call my garden *home*. I have been digging out foxtail, pulling it and having words with it here and there, telling it to *go and live someplace else*. Bindweed and foxtail are the bane of the Midwest gardener.

When I look at my garden in July, I feel there is no rhyme or reason to anything. I am not a garden or landscape designer, but instead I put plants wherever there might be a space or where I think they will grow nicely. I do know to plant the taller plants to the back of the garden, to add a shrub or two for structure, but the other plants – well, that is another story. I call it a *wild woman's garden* and that describes it perfectly (except for the @#&% foxtail and bindweed!).

I like all flowers. Wherever a flower pops up or chooses to grow I usually let it live there, until there are too many and then I share with others. The larkspur blooms prolifically late spring through July, and I let them re-seed each year, as this is a favorite colorful flower. I also let a few daisies and lemon balm re-seed, but do not let them run over the garden. They all become *pass-along* plants.

> ***In joy or sadness, flowers are our constant friends.***
> -Kozuko Okakura

The garlic I planted last October is ready to dig up in July. It wintered over beautifully covered with four inches of old straw. Now it will be pulled up and laid on a flat surface in the garage to cure out for several weeks. I leave the garage door open for the breezes to blow around it on dry days, and after several weeks I will hang it with four to six bulbs per bunch. Otherwise I use as I need directly from the garden, one or two bulbs at a time. I have never had luck with garlic lasting more than two or three months once it's pulled, so I end up fermenting and pickling garlic cloves, which are delicious.

SUMMER TEA

I put together a variety of summer herbs and flowers: passion-flower, elderflower, borage, a little orange peel, lemon balm, spearmint and add hot water to steep 2 to 4 hours in a jar with a lid. Strain and serve over ice (I make sure all the flowers chosen are edible).

GARDEN CANDLE

In an empty quart jar I add a cup or two of fine sand. Into the sand I stick a votive candle or tea light and sit the candlelights along a walkway or in a garden (away from dried plant material) and light when guests arrive. I check on the candles often. When done using, I blow out, screw lids on tightly and either leave sit in the garden or store in garage until ready to use again.

★★★

IN THE KITCHEN IN JULY

Don't eat anything your great-grandmother
would not recognize as food.
-Michael Pollen

HERB POTATO SALAD
Add or subtract to this basic recipe:
8 medium organic potatoes, peeled and cooked
1 c. salad dressing or mayonnaise
2 T. vinegar
1/3 c. milk
1 tsp. Dijon mustard
2 T. finely chopped onion or green onions
1 tsp. fresh thyme, stripped from stem and chopped fine
1 ½ tsp. dried dill weed or fresh dill, snipped fine
1 tsp. salt
½ tsp. white or black pepper

Cook potatoes until almost done but still firm in lightly salted
water. Drain. Let cool completely. In small bowl, combine all other
ingredients to desired taste. Pour mixture over potatoes and toss

gently to coat. Cover and chill several hours, preferably overnight, to let flavors draw through.

ELDERBERRIES

The elderflowers are used to make a champagne which is delicious, but I know if I take the flowers there will be no berries for the birds or me. Yet the flowers are truly a delicacy. I dry some flowers to use in hot wildflower tea in the winter.

The elderberries are common along the roadsides, and they ripen to a dark purple/black color in late July into August in the Midwest. The common elderberry should not be ingested until it has been cooked, as the seed is toxic raw. The stem is poisonous also. I have heard of elderberry pie, but I cannot imagine eating it, as there are tons of seeds – a big seed in each berry.

I am careful when collecting elderberry along country roads. If there are crop fields or pasture nearby the chances are high it has been sprayed with chemicals. I have planted my own patch now, and it is growing. Elderberry is very important for my winter medicine.

When I make elderberry jelly, I clip the whole heads of the elderberries as short as I can and put the heads in a stainless steel pot with a little filtered water and steam (simmer, not boil). I then strain the juice to make jelly or syrup. I follow a berry jelly recipe on the Sure Jell pectin recipe sheet or an apple jelly recipe. Either works.

After jelly is made I do a hot water bath for the filled jars to ensure a tight seal. If not sealed properly, mold can form on the top. I remember as a kid, if there was mold on the top of the jelly we were told to just scoop it off and throw it away; the rest was OK to eat. Today I know better. Mold grows tentacles down and throughout whatever it sits on. I err on the side of caution always.

If I am too busy when the elderberries ripen the end of July, I will clip the heads and put in big baggies (I double bag) and freeze until January or a slower time to work with. I believe all food is best used fresh, as any preserving by canning, freezing, or drying can decrease some of its goodness.

Elderberry jelly is quite a delicacy. A spoonful of jelly on a piece of toast on a cold January morning will take me right back to summertime and the elderberries ripening.

To make Elderberry juice:

Harvest the heads where the berries have all turned dark (ripened). *Do not wash.* Cut off the small clusters that make up the big cluster, removing any fleshy stem. I fill a large stainless-steel pot with the sprigs of berries and add one cup of filtered water to begin steaming. I cover and steam on low-medium heat for 20-30 minutes, then remove from heat and let cool down with the lid on. After cooling, I mash out the juice from the tiny berries. I strain the juice twice through an extra fine mesh strainer. A potato ricer helps get out all the precious usable juice. The juice can be used to make jelly, syrup or tonic or the juice can be frozen for later use. When I don't have enough elderberry juice, I add aronia or blackberry juice.

SIMPLE ELDERBERRY SYRUP / ELIXIR
Fresh *(or dried)* **Elderberries**
Water as needed
Spices to taste: Cardamom, Clove, Lemon/Lime/Orange Peel, Cinnamon, Allspice, Nutmeg, Ginger

Make elderberry juice. If using dried elderberries, soak them overnight (use soaking water as part of syrup).
If using fresh ginger, grate small and squeeze out juice from grated ginger and add to elder juice. Measure juice and add ½-part raw

organic honey. If desired, also add Brandy (1:1 or ½:1 with juice). Store in refrigerator. I take a tablespoon a day for wellness. If making large quantity, freeze extra juice and add honey/brandy when transitioning to refrigerator for use. Will keep longer with brandy added.

ELDERBERRY JELLY

Elderberry jelly is a delicacy. A spoonful on a piece of toast on a cold January morning will take me back to summertime when the elderberries were ripening.

I buy a package of powdered *Sure-Jell* and read directions inside. Since elderberry is not listed, I follow the directions for Boysenberry/Dewberry cooked jelly recipe.

Tip: I have made all kinds of jams and jellies in the past, and once in a while one will not set up like a jelly should. At that point, I can decide if I want to use it as a syrup or remake into a jelly that will set up. This is extra work, but worth the effort. There are instructions on the sheet for jelly that doesn't set up. I eliminate doing the trial batch and do remainder of batch process, and on the second try it always sets up.

This recipe will make 7 cups jelly. I like to put into one-half cup jars and add to gift baskets at holiday time. Jars can be purchased at hardware or big box stores. After jelly is in the jars, use hot water bath (covering jars with water and lid) for 5 to 10 minutes. This ensures a tight seal on the filled jars and they are ready for storage. The jars will store up to a year on a shelf. Once opened, they must be refrigerated.

ELDERBERRY

Summer isn't here until the elderberry blooms,
And summer doesn't end until the berries are ripe.
-old saying (source unknown)

Grandmother Elder has been a close friend for the last thirty years of my life. I have always been able to find her along fencerows, next to a pasture or in a meadow, and gathering berries has been a long-standing ritual.

Euell Gibbon's popular 1962 book, *Stalking the Wild Asparagus,* became a favorite book of mine and put me on a path of foraging and learning about the wild plants, including wild elderberry. I was intrigued by the valuable information in his book, and later when I gained more knowledge about the medicine of elder, I knew she and I would have a close connection.

Elder is my plant ally. I call her my *flu shot in a bottle.* On October first, I am ready to begin my winter ritual of taking a tablespoon of elderberry tonic each morning, and I continue until April first, as it is shown to be very effective at preventing winter colds and flu. The pioneers called elderberry the *poor man's medicine chest,* as they believed it could cure almost anything. In France, it is referred to as the *House Pharmacy*.

There are several varieties of elder, and it must be identified correctly. It is important to note that the seeds are toxic until heated/cooked. The wild species I find and have planted in my yard is *Sambucus nigra* (also called *Sambucus canadensis)* or Black Elderberry. The little berries are blue/black in color and quite easy to identify. They are on a flat umbel – a flower head the shape of a dinner plate. Native Americans traditionally made tea from elderberry to treat respiratory infections. Research studies have found elderberry to be packed with antioxidants, and it fights bacteria and overcomes viruses. It is high in flavonoids which disrupt a virus's ability to replicate and is interesting to note that studies have shown elderberry to be effective against eight different influenza viruses, including H1N1.

In some parts of the world elder grows as a tree, but in the Midwest, it is usually a community of shrubs about 6 to 8 feet tall. Elder likes well-drained soil so her feet are not wet for long periods of time.

When I moved to my current location in the woods, I planted elder not far from my house in a place she would get at least a half a day of sunshine. Being close by, I visit her often and can easily collect the berries when ripe, year after year. The plant was a "sucker" or a starter plant growing alongside the mother. I pampered her for the first two years, and the third year she produced sixteen huge umbels of flowers the size of dinner plates. When the flowers turned into dark berries, I clipped off the big umbels of berries with gratitude. She is now eight feet tall. I have staked her for support, and once the berries set on I cover elder completely with black netting from a fabric store, securing the sides and ends with pinch clothespins. The netting works well, keeping the berries safe from the birds, who would otherwise be feasting before I could. Elder is a joy, and I tell her so often – she responds well. Soon she will have babies shooting up from the ground beside her, and this will one day be a small community of elders.

Elder begins to ripen mid- to late-July. It all depends on the summer we are having, and of course global warming may change everything. I like to record each year when the different fruits ripen and can compare this information year after year.

In horticulture, the elder leaves are boiled, cooled and strained to make a natural insecticidal spray.

Elderberry flowers can be used to make a champagne-like wine. If picking the flowers, I use them sparingly for the wine or dried for a tea. The champagne is delicious and medicinal, but if there are no flowers on the shrub, there will be no berries. The berries can be used as a syrup, elixir or jelly. I find it takes a lot of berries to make a little juice.

The berries can be dried or frozen for later use. I prefer to use fresh whenever possible as I believe the berries are at their prime and have more good constituents in them. If drying, the berries need to be removed from the head. I use only dark, healthy-looking berries. If I find I am too busy to process the berries, I put the whole berry heads into gallon zipper plastic bags and double-bag, then freeze to process later in the year when I am not as busy.

Elder juice can be used as a dye. Until recently, French school-children used ink made from elderberries. I enjoy dyeing silk scarves using elderberries and other plant material.

Folklore says to not burn the elder branches. The old saying was, *"Elder is the Lady's Tree, burn it not or cursed ye be."* Celtic lore says the spirits of the forest dwell in the hollow wood of the elder tree. Taking any part of the elder requires making an offering and asking permission or risking the Elder Mother's wrath.

QUEEN ANNE'S LACE

Queen Anne's Lace is a beautiful native wildflower blooming in June and July. It is considered an invasive weed by many people. It is also known as Wild Carrot, and the taproot is like a carrot and can be eaten the first year. In the Midwest, Queen Anne's lace is seen along roadsides this time of year. Wildflowers are beautiful, and this is one of my favorites. I like to clip the blossoms to press and dry for notecards or to have fresh in a vase to enjoy on my table.

Handling Queen Anne's lace can cause dermatitis (a rash) with some people. The seedpods are quite distinctive and help to identify the plant correctly. The pods resemble a bird nest. The flat flower head pulls itself inward as it dries, creating a caged "nest" that holds the seeds.

However, as beautiful as it is, there are cautions with this plant. First, I am sure to identify it correctly as Queen Anne's lace as there is a look-alike plant that is deadly poisonous. To identify, I look closely at the flat cluster of tiny creamy-colored flowers searching for a single dark burgundy colored spot (a floret) in the middle of the flowerhead. Folklore says the plant was named after Queen Anne of England. She was a needlewoman who made lace, and when she pricked her finger, a single drop of blood fell onto the lace. This is the dark spot in the center of the flower head. The flower itself resembles delicate lace.

The look-alike plant of Queen Anne's lace is poison hemlock. It is extremely important to know the differences between these plants. False parsley is another look alike. Many plants have look-alikes in the natural world. The stems on Queen Anne's lace are hairy, whereas on hemlock the stems are smooth.

When I find a patch of Queen Anne's lace, I bring a bouquet into the house to admire and watch the flower heads gradually turn into the bird nest seedpods. It is a beautiful plant indeed.

QUEEN ANNE'S LACE JELLY
Has a delicious light floral taste.
Note: First identify Queen Anne's Lace correctly. I normally collect the first week of July in my area. Read all instructions first before gathering the blooms to make the jelly so all supplies are on hand.

To make infusion for jelly:

2 packed cups of heads (approximately 20 heads of fresh blooms, not older blooms)
4 c. almost boiling water

I use a half-gallon jar for the heads and pour the hot water over, punching down and stirring with a wood spoon. Cover with lid. Let set to steep and cool down 4 hours. Strain two times with super fine small strainer and cotton cloth, being careful not to disrupt the sediment in bottom of jar. Leave behind about ¼ c. of sediment if present. Toss the wilted heads in compost.

Have six 4 oz. jelly jars with two-piece lids sterilized and ready or eight 2 oz. jars, which are a smaller size and great for giving away. Set jars on a cookie sheet (with sides) lined with clean towel.

To make jelly:
3 cups strained infusion
2 T. lemon juice (from a fresh lemon – not bottled)
1 pkg. Sure Jell powdered fruit pectin

Put all in a large stainless steel pan, stir and bring to a rolling boil. Add 4 c. sugar and boil 1 minute longer. Remove from heat. If any foam on top, skim off with large metal spoon. Ladle into jars. Wipe rims of jars and put lids on and screw down tightly. Use hot water bath (covering jars with water and lid) for 5 to 10 minutes. Remove jars carefully and let rest 24 hours.

BLACK-EYED SUSAN

❧

(RUDBECKIA HIRTA)

he Black-Eyed Susans are blooming abundantly by the first of July, blanketing the meadows and dotting the roadside ditches. I eagerly anticipate their appearance and watch for them, as they seem to signal summer is here to stay.

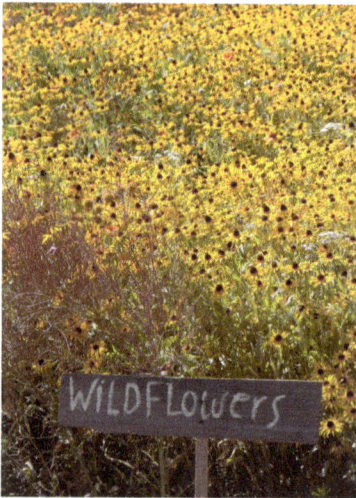

The daisy-like flowers are a cheery golden yellow with a brownish-black center, and there are several varieties that grow in the wild. I am smitten by the smaller ones that have a bloom the size of a quarter or less, as many are a silver dollar in size. I never give a second look to the tame varieties in pots at the garden center – it is the wild ones that I fall in love with every summer.

Insects love the flowers too. I notice the birds eating the seed from the heads in the wintertime, so I do not cut them back until early spring. The Susans bloom from late June to October here in the Midwest and grace my table often throughout their long blooming season. The sturdy cut flowers last a full week with water in a vase, and sometimes that vase is an old blue glass canning jar and other times a small crock.

In traditional Native American medicine, the Black-Eyed Susan was used as a remedy for colds and flu and a poultice for snakebite.

NOTE: *I have found black-eyed Susans can cause irritation to my arms when rubbing against it, but that also happens when I handle tomato plants in my garden. Now I wear gloves and a long-sleeved shirt when I collect my flowers.*

August

THE VIEW FROM MY WINDOW

Every day may not be good,
but there is something good in every day.
-Unknown

The land is dry and sunburned and the leaves are curling on the trees. Meadow grasses are turning brown and plants are making haste to release seed before completely drying up. It is a typical August in the Midwest.

Once in a great while we have a green August, but most years August is desert-like. The creeks and ponds are dry now. Birds and insects hide themselves during the heat of the day, and I find a shade tree to sit under with a tall glass of cold herbal tea. I water the few plants still wanting to produce.

My body is weary from the gardening chores by the time August arrives, but there is still much to do. The zucchini continues to produce, and this is the vegetable mainstay of a stir-fry I like to make during the summer. I never tire of zucchini bread and zucchini brownies, and extra zucchini is shredded and frozen and whole zucchinis are given away.

I enjoy seeing what is growing outside, and I walk in the gardens in the early morning when it is cooler. Being outside in the yard is no longer as pleasurable as it was in the springtime. Everything looks tired and tattered this time of year, including me. The only plant surviving extra well is the ragweed, and it seems to laugh in my face when I am outside, as if to tell me *you had better stay inside today*. But I venture out, doing the work needing to be done, and then when ragweed has said *hello* to me, I must go inside for the rest of the day. It seems unfair to me, as much as I love being with my plants and out in nature. But it is the end of August, and I know I must be inside when ragweed is blooming and the pollen is blowing in the wind.

Everyone I see this month seems to have the same thing to say during these *dog days* of summer, and that is, *"I am really, really ready for autumn to arrive."* The change to cooler weather will be welcome, and already I am noticing the mornings becoming a bit cooler, or maybe it is wishful thinking. The late summer work still needs to be done – freezing, canning and drying of the fruits, veggies and herbs. The tomatoes are growing well, and there are slices on my noon and evening plates. I am still fond of the little yellow pear tomatoes of my childhood and plant two every year, and they produce enough to satisfy my eating out of the hand right in the garden patch. Pesto is made and frozen to take me through the winter months.

> *He handed me a big tomato, scarlet, fragrant, less than twelve hours from its vine. "That colour is the sunlight," he told me. "The skins of fruits and vegetables are subtly charged with the properties of the life-giving sun. Eat it and you will understand magic."*
> -Henri Carpentier

August is typically known as the month of stone fruits – the fruits with pits ripen this month. The trees produce abundantly and the markets are full of stone fruits. My old peach tree faithfully produces, some years more than others. The spring pink peach blossoms were glorious and then the fruit set. This old-fashioned white peach tree was given to me by my mom as a pit (stone). She saved it when she canned her white peaches given to her by an old friend. I have canned peaches and thrown out the stones/pits into a compost pile and little peach trees have grown from them, and I have shared many of the little trees. The white peaches come from old stock, are winter hardy, and the fruit is less acidic than a yellow peach and much sweeter, like eating candy.

I buy a few organic yellow peaches at market and slice them to dry in my dehydrator. They are a quick snack in the winter, or if one has an upset stomach, a dried peach slice will help it go away.

The garlic chives are now blooming large white heads, which I clip to put into white wine vinegar, sometimes adding a sprig of basil. After infusing for six to eight weeks, this will become the base for a tasty olive oil salad dressing I make which visitors rave over. I leave many blossoms for the bees to enjoy, and those blossoms will go to seed, ensuring a lot of baby plants next spring to give away. Before all the seeds drop to the ground, I clip the seed heads and put in a fall bouquet of other dried materials from nature. I love having garlic chives in my herb garden.

The first part of August I am still gathering bouquets of the little black-eyed Susans for my kitchen table, using an old salt-glazed stoneware crock as a vase for a simple country look. The Susans run wild in my meadow and garden edges, and I enjoy both the large and small varieties, but the tiny little Susans with flowers about the size of a quarter are my favorites. I cannot resist them and have given seed heads to many friends who have stopped by my shop or home and admired them.

Both the large and small black-eyed Susans grow in my garden. They often appear where I least expect them and certainly not where I planted them, because I didn't plant them at all. Seed blows around the meadow or comes from the birds and then I have plants, here and there and everywhere. These plants require no care, deer leave them alone, they reseed themselves and grow and bloom for all to enjoy. The seed heads are beautiful in a fall arrangement.

My kitchen table has been graced by the very last of the Queen Anne's lace flowers showing off in an antique blue quart canning jar. I collect a few of the seed heads, which I call "cages" and some call "bird nests." The spent flower folds into itself, forming a "cage" look, and the seeds ripen to be scattered to the wind later in the season. I add the seed heads to autumn wreaths.

There are annual and perennial plants blooming in August, and I water to extend their season of beauty. The morning glory wraps around the birdhouse on the porch post on the east side, greeting me every morning. The hyacinth bean and clematis share a trellis, zinnia and cosmos bloom where I planted them, the three miniature roses bloom profusely all summer long, and the geraniums sit in their pots by the front entry to my porch. Folklore says that a red geranium by the front door keeps evil away.

The birdbaths are filled often, and I enjoy watching birds take afternoon baths, cooling off in the summer heat and splashing around to their hearts' delight. When I lived next to cornfields and the ponds and creeks were dry in August, I would fill an old galvanized tub in the evening for the deer, raccoon, wild turkeys and whatever else might be roaming at night and need a drink. Each morning I could tell animals had found a cool drink and perhaps a bath. Now that I live in the woods by a watershed lake, I do not worry about the large animals needing water as they can walk to the lake close by.

In a walk through the meadow on a late August day, I gather items to make a fall bouquet – something I do often during the year and every autumn for sure. I find a few grasses and flowers are beginning to release their seeds, and I watch for the *stick-tights* and *Bidens* (also called *Spanish Needles*) which adhere to my clothing – I want to stay clear of those. It is Nature's ingenious way of spreading the seed and planting weeds and flowers *hither and yon*. I marvel at Nature every time I take a walk and watch the progress of the seasons.

The end of August is a good time to take a walk and collect a few treasures from nature to enjoy throughout the upcoming months. I am always intrigued and amazed at what I find when I go walking.

> *When summer opens, I see how fast it matures,*
> *and fear it will be short;*
> *but after the heat of July and August, I am reconciled,*
> *like one who has had his swing, to the cool of autumn.*
> -Ralph Waldo Emerson

THE FULL MOON IN AUGUST

I enjoy the history and folklore of each month's full moons and consider moon lore important to pass along to our children and grandchildren to keep them immersed in nature. Creating full moon celebrations of our own is a good way to make new traditions for our families.

The *Green Corn Moon* was a popular name for the August full moon, as the corn is ripening in August and corn was a staple for Native Americans and early settlers. Many tribes celebrated with a corn festival at full moon time. In folklore, a prediction of winter was: *If corn shucks are thicker and tougher than usual, the winter ahead will be hard.*

The *Full Sturgeon Moon* was another name given to the August moon by the fishing tribes since sturgeon, large fish of the Great Lakes and other major bodies of water, were most readily caught during this month.

A few tribes knew the August moon as the *Full Red Moon* because as the Moon rises it appears reddish through the sultry haze of an August night.

The Osage tribe name for August moon is *Yellow Flower Moon* as the yellow flowers blooming in August are black-eyed Susans, golden-rod, sunflower and partridge pea.

IN THE GARDEN IN AUGUST

EAT WATERMELON SEEDS

Watermelon is an appealing and cooling treat on a hot August day. It is considered both vegetable and fruit, and it is said to be one of the most healing foods of summer, as it is both hydrating and cooling. Eating watermelon can help to cool the body during a heatstroke. In the South, many people pickle watermelon rind to use for poor digestion. It has been said the rind can be dried and used in a tea for loss of voice or sore throat, and is good for dehydration and hot flashes. The pink to red watermelon has more health benefits than a yellow watermelon. We grew up being told to "spit out the seeds," but research shows the seeds are good for us. They are a powerful source of minerals and Omega-3 fatty acids. The seeds are also a powerful kidney cleanser and a strong diuretic. Chinese stores sell flavored watermelon seeds.

GOURD CRAZY

I admit it – I am gourd crazy! I go off the deep end when it comes to gourds. I love gourds undecorated, just the way they grew from

Mother Earth. I know some people love to decorate them in bright colors, but I like them to be in their natural state, and if adorned, I prefer the decorations to be from Nature too.

I buy the big gourds I cannot grow where I live, and grow the little gourds myself. In the early spring, I plant gourd seeds in starter pots so when they are ready to transplant outside they already have a good start. The different varieties must be planted away from each other, as they will cross-pollinate, and I like to save the seeds to plant again another year. Each year they are planted, I choose a different spot to help control squash bugs.

At the end of the garden I put up a trellis or hog wire fencing with a steel post for support, and this is where I plant the little hard-shelled gourds. These gourds need a long growing season – the larger the gourd, the longer the growing season. The bushel gourd will take 4 to 5 months to mature on the vine. The big gourds do not grow well where seasons are shorter. Once they are picked, the larger the gourd the longer the drying time also – up to a year for the big ones. After picking, I leave the gourds untouched to dry out so they can be used as decoration. To dry out, they should not be stored where they might freeze. If the gourd is pierced, nicked or cracked it cannot be used, as it will rot. I store my gourds in the garage, which stays above freezing. The tiniest gourds mature in three months and then dry out in another three months; however, I dry them longer (six to nine months).

Gourds are a delight and wonder of nature, and a use can be found for each one. I especially love the miniature *dancing gourds* and the *egg gourds*. History shows Native Americans used gourds as collecting containers, and later the early settlers did as well. The longer gourds were used as dippers for water.

I am completely enamored with the tiniest gourds, called *dancing gourds* or *spinner gourds*. I first saw them at a craft show and then my best friend grew them. After I moved away, she sent me a ditty bag appliquéd in wool with the word GOURDS and filled with the tiny gourds. I treasure this gift from her heart and her garden – she knows I love the plants on Mother Earth. Since then I have grown my own little gourds. The gourds can be strung on brown hemp cording as a necklace, and other items such as dried whole nutmegs, rose hips, seeds and even stones (drilled for jewelry making) can be added.

TIP: *AFTER THE GOURDS HAVE THOROUGHLY DRIED THEY WILL HAVE developed a splotchy look or residue on them, which is a mold and is natural. This gives the wonderful mottled look as they cure. I rub the hard, thin layer of mold off with a small piece of rough steel wool or a stainless steel "scrubby" in water, then rinse the gourds in vinegar water. Once thoroughly dry they can be waxed. I sometimes use a brown paste wax on them or a clear one that leaves them in their natural color, as I believe Mother Nature knows what she is doing when she chooses the colors for decorating the earth.*

IN THE KITCHEN IN AUGUST

Zucchini is prolific, and my garden is overrun with it come August. I use it in stir-fries, sliced thin as noodles, dried and seasoned as a snack, in casseroles, for pickle spears, in relishes, and I give it away. I enjoy zucchini and plant it every year. I remember to change locations in my garden each year when I plant it to help keep the pesky squash bugs at bay. By the end of August, the squash bugs usually win. And by then I have had my fill of zucchini!

ZUCCHINI RELISH
5 c. grated zucchini
5 c. grated cucumber
6 onions
3 green peppers
1 red pepper
2 tsp. canning salt

Use a food processor or grater. The veggies should be in small relish size pieces. Mix well in a big bowl. Let set 1-2 hours and drain through a colander and then through a strainer, or a fine cheesecloth or cotton dishtowel could be laid in the strainer. Squeeze out and drain. Set aside.

In a large stainless-steel pan make the brine:
2 c. apple cider vinegar
4 c. sugar
2 tsp. mustard seed
1 tsp. celery seed
1 tsp. turmeric

BOIL THIS BRINE FOR 5-7 MINUTES. THEN ADD THE drained zucchini mixture. Mix together and bring almost to a boil, then remove from heat. Put into pint jars with 2- piece lids for sealing. Hot water bath for 10 minutes. Makes 6-7 pint.

PIZZA ZUCCHINI CASSEROLE
Kids like this. Tastes like pizza but uses up the extra zucchini and they will never know.
4 to 5 c. shredded unpeeled zucchini
½ tsp. salt
2 large eggs or 3 medium eggs, beaten
1 lb. ground beef
½ to 1 c. onion, finely chopped
1 can (15 oz.) Italian tomato sauce or spaghetti sauce
1-2 tsp. All Purpose herb mix (in January chapter)
1/2 to 1 medium green pepper, finely chopped
1 c. shredded cheddar cheese, divided
2 c. shredded mozzarella cheese, divided

Put grated zucchini and salt in big bowl and let stand 10 minutes, then drain and squeeze out excess moisture. Combine drained zucchini with eggs and half the cheeses. Press into 9x13 greased pan. Bake 20 minutes at 350 degrees.

In large saucepan, cook beef well, crumbling into small pieces. Then add onion and green pepper. Cook until almost done. Add sauce and herb mix. Spoon over zucchini mixture. Sprinkle with remaining cheeses. Bake 25 minutes longer at 350 degrees. Makes 6-8 servings.

SUNFLOWERS

❦

The sunflower is mine, in a way.
-Vincent Van Gogh

Sunflowers grow in the fields and along the roadside in ditches and meadows in August. When the sunflowers are in full bloom, I know we are close to the end of summer. I like them all – from cultivated sunflowers to the wild blooms painting the meadows bright yellow. I now live in the Sunflower State of Kansas and enjoy the sunflowers to their fullest when August comes around.

The sunflower is thought to have originated in Peru and Mexico and was one of the first plants to be cultivated in the United States. Native Americans used the sunflower for hundreds of years as food and other parts of the plant for dye pigment.

The nutritional value of sunflower seed is substantial, being high in Vitamin E, magnesium and selenium. It is said to calm nerves by eating the seeds, but I also think looking at a sunflower in full bloom or clustered in a field is calming. Studies have shown that sunflower seeds can lower high blood pressure, prevent migraines, and reduce the risk of heart attack and stroke.

Bees are responsible for the pollination of sunflowers. The seeds are used for cooking oil, for fuel, and as a healthy food for people and birds.

Bouquets of beautiful varieties of ornamental sunflowers can be found at Farmers' Markets around the country, and I always buy a few for my table when at the Market. The variety I like the best produces huge seed heads and is called *Mammoth Russian*. Dried heads are pretty in a big wooden trencher and can be fed to the birds outside when the weather changes. I use the purchased organic raw sunflower seed hearts on salads, in baking cookies and in trail mix. The regular salted whole seed is known best for its snack appeal. I picked the little black-eyed Susans in July, and now at the end of August, bouquets of wild sunflowers adorn my table and bring their sunshine into my life.

September

THE VIEW FROM MY WINDOW

For man, Autumn is a time of harvest, of gathering together,
for nature it is a time of sowing, of scattering around.
- Edwin Way Teale

Welcome September, my dear old friend!

The blessed rains have come to our parched earth. It is the song of September and the rain is music to my ear, heart and soul. Summer will soon be but a memory. Autumn Equinox arrives at the time of the full September moon this year, the apples are ready to be picked, and I am looking forward to the pumpkins and the sights and scents of the autumn season. The plant roots, many of which are used for medicine and food, are sending their nutrients downward, preparing for the winter ahead. I'll dig a few roots later after the first hard frost, but most I will leave for their long winter's nap. The leaves on the trees are beginning to change color, and a few are letting go, falling to the earth. I pick up a few leaves to press in a book. I love searching for and finding the heart-shaped leaves, but all are beautiful to me. I am a tree hugger!

247

The art of being happy lies in the power of extracting happiness from common things.
-Henry Ward Beecher

SEPTEMBER IS THE GATEWAY TO AUTUMN, MY FAVORITE of all the seasons. My senses are filled with the colors, sights, scents, and sounds of September. My mindset is changing, and I want to dig out the sweaters, bake the yummy fall foods, buy a pumpkin, light a cinnamon and clove scented candle and put out the gourd garland that I will hang from the fireplace mantle.

I am keeping an ear to the skies when I am outside, listening for the Canadian geese honking their ancient song of fall migration, announcing they are getting ready for the change of seasons too. Now with global warming they are sometimes staying in the Midwest all winter long.

The annual harvesting of apples has begun. I wish every yard had an apple tree and knew the rewards of this wonderful tree all year long. The three apple trees planted on my daughter's land have begun to produce a few apples, but in years to come they will produce more, and the apples will be greatly anticipated and appreciated when Autumn comes around each year. Last year I planted a Liberty apple tree not far from my house. It is an heirloom apple that resists the apple cedar rust. I protect it from the deer as much as I can, and coddle it as I wait for it to grow big enough to produce an apple or two, or perhaps a bushel full or more.

But for now, I content myself by visiting a nearby orchard on a Sunday afternoon where I pick organic apples to bring home and sip freshly pressed apple cider while savoring the autumn day. At home, I dry apple slices for winter snacking, make applesauce, cider muffins, apple butter and the usual apple pies and apple crisp. It is important to connect to the earth each season of the year, celebrating what Mother Earth gives us, being grateful for her gifts, and living in the fullness of these September days.

The really hot days of the summer season will soon be behind us, but even a few 90-degree days will not last long now, and the cooler days will be forthcoming. I look forward to the foggy mornings September brings, and I shift gears with the coming Equinox. Life patterns create changes in us this season, and we become more focused on preparing for the next season ahead – winter. The days are getting shorter, and we lose around fifteen minutes of daylight each week this month.

I linger outside a little longer on these beautiful warm September days, putting my bare feet on Mother Earth, absorbing the magnetic forces within her. I close my eyes and pull those forces up through my toes and through my body. Barefoot, I collect the last of the harvest, gathering seeds for next season to plant, and eating freshly picked little yellow tomatoes from the vine.

A favorite fall pastime is gathering grasses and seedpods to adorn a stoneware crock in my family room, bringing autumn inside with me. Bringing nature inside is something I have always loved doing, and I believe being a *gatherer* is in my DNA. My ancestral grandmothers gathered food from the wild at first, and then from gardens as we do today. I gather everything. I carry an antique basket with me, collecting small items I find. Today I may find a feather from a bluebird, an intricately made fallen wasp nest, a rock with mica sparkling in the sun, a lichen-covered small branch, a beautiful dried seed head of a wild sunflower, roses drying on the stem, or the sculptural seed pods of wild vines. I find the tansy and clip off dried tansy blossoms, once golden yellow but now a rusty brown color. In September the goldenrod is in full bloom, and I gather a bouquet for an old quart-size brown crock jar. The little brown crock jar is wonderful with a little chip on the top rim (none of us are perfect) and a wide opening at the top, big enough to slip in a skinny water glass to hold the water for the flowers and protect the old crock.

A little further down the lane, I discover for the first time a big patch of wild hops, meandering here and there and almost covering a mid-size tree. I wind and wrap the long vines into beautiful wreaths, a few into door hangings and the smaller pieces I will dry. Every year I find new treasures along my country lane or in the woods, being mindful and aware as I walk. The crows are noisily cawing overhead, and I talk to them. And then, close to my house, I stand under an old tree that sings to me in its gentle swaying. I discovered this tree one day when I heard a distinctive sound I could not identify – like otherworldly music. I walked closer to the sound, looked up and saw the branches moving ever so slowly, and heard actual soft music coming from the top of the tree. I turned my head this way and that, trying to figure out if it really was coming from the tree, and it was. I witnessed this magical experience three separate times this summer, and now I call this tree my *magical musical tree,* and I sing its praises.

> *Savor the beauty in life and return to it often,*
> *It will be the mark you leave upon the world.*
> -unknown

My antique baskets, crocks and old wooden bowls are always filled with the gifts from nature and Mother Earth. These small found items from the prairie and woods fill my heart and soul. They are natural, interesting to look at and provide lessons for learning – unexpected, simple treasures.

This last weekend, daughter and I gathered wild *Artemisia*, fall grasses and goldenrod in the meadow towards the lake. We also found *Bidens*, blue Vervain, ironweed and mountain mint. Each time we walk we find another surprise like wild indigo seed pod stems, and we mark the wild herbs and scatter a few of the seeds in the area, hoping more plants will grow.

> *I cannot endure to waste anything as precious*
> *as autumn sunshine by staying in the house.*
> *So, I spend almost all the daylight hours in the open air.*
> – Nathaniel Hawthorne

I will gather a few milkweed stalks after frost, but first I wait for the seeds to scatter along the roadsides, re-seeding for a new crop next year. I watch for the chrysalis and the caterpillar of the monarch butterfly on the stalks. The wild milkweed is the food of the monarchs, and there are so few of these beautiful insects left in the world due to the intense pesticide/herbicide spraying of fields, meadows and roadsides. How sad it would be to live in a world without honeybees or butterflies.

Many home gardeners are now planting the common wild milk-weed in their private gardens to help the monarchs. It is a beautiful plant in the garden, and the common milkweed is not so common anymore, although some years I see more milkweed than other years. It is significant that gardeners are planting the milkweed in their private gardens today. We need to be the protectors of wildlife – not the destroyers.

The garden has gone wild by the end of September, as it does each and every year. I let it roam at will now, with vines going every which way, and the paths are no longer paths, as the plants reach for one another in a warm embrace. I find one more zucchini I need to pick, which was hidden under the big leaves, the last of the okra pods I will dry for winter wreaths, and under more leaves I find little dancing gourds hiding.

The tomatoes and cucumbers need picking again and are coming to the end of their prolific production for the season. Extra tomatoes will be frozen and cucumbers made into more bread and butter pickles. The days, nights and moon are dictating their growth these last late summer days.

September is the time of year when I consider which of the annuals I need to overwinter, as they will need to be potted up to bring inside. The scented geraniums come inside after pruning, and I will root the clippings to gift to friends. I will clip a few sprigs of coleus to root and start in a new pot. The mini-leaf basil, sometimes called *Boxwood Basil*, was planted in a pot and not directly into the ground this year. I clipped the bottom branches to make it into a topiary, and it is lovely – this being one of my favorite things I did this summer. As I clipped and shaped the topiary, I collected the tiny leaves to use on pizza, in scrambled eggs, or in a salad. The leaves are so small they do not need to be chopped, and the flavor is excellent. I will also freeze basil leaves by laying them on a paper towel, rolling the towel up tightly, and placing in double sandwich bags. Sometimes I put the leaves into an ice cube tray and pour olive oil over to freeze, and this works best by freezing a layer of olive oil, then adding basil leaves and a bit of oil, and after the middle layer is frozen I top it off with more olive oil. It gives summer flavor to dishes in the upcoming winter season.

September days bring misty and sometimes foggy mornings, warm afternoons and cooler evenings. On this September night, the full moon above is lighting my path in the garden, turning the garden into moonlit shadows of various shapes. The chirping of crickets is a soothing lullaby. If the temperature is above 75 degrees, the cicadas' songs begin around sunset. The barred owl is talking to a neighboring owl in my woods tonight. The night is alive with these wild songs – a gentle way to end the day. I love the coming of autumn.

THE FULL MOON IN SEPTEMBER

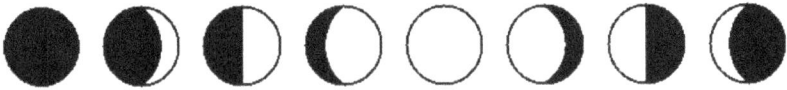

The September full moon has been called the *Full Corn Moon*, as it is when corn is beginning to be harvested. Most often, the September full moon is called the *Harvest Moon*. It is a time for gathering in the final harvest, storing away for winter, and collecting the last of what the garden is producing before the frost comes in October. The weather remains fairly calm and peaceful in September, allowing the autumn harvest and work to be finished.

September Full Moon
Bright in the moon the autumn wood
Its crimson scarf unrolled,
And the trees like a splendid army stood
In a panoply of gold!
-Henry Wadsworth Longfellow (Musings, 1825)

IN THE GARDEN IN SEPTEMBER

Fair on September first, fair for the entire month.
- old adage

*M*y garden is looking worn out and used up by the end of September, and I am feeling that way too. The garlic chives are setting seed, the cosmos are still blooming their hearts out, the miniature roses never cease to amaze me, and even the lavender is sending up a stalk of flowers here and there after their flush of blooms in June. The last of the onions and potatoes are dug up, cured and stored. The clean-up of the garden will start soon, although I keep it to a minimum, as I leave the seed heads of many plants and weeds for the birds now. The gardens are getting ready for a well-deserved rest, and I am too. I will soon miss seeing what is budded, what is blooming, or what needs attention. All will be put to rest.

At the end of September, I look into the woods – the understory vines and small bushes are beginning to drop leaves, making it easier for me to see further into the woods. I see a squirrel scampering about, perhaps a rabbit hiding away from the sharp eyes of an owl, and now and then I see quail, or a deer coming closer, or some other creature stirring up the cushioning blanket of dried leaves on the earth. There are many Osage oranges, also called hedge apples, littering the earth under the mother tree. Plants in my garden and weeds on the perimeters are setting seed.

Walking in the lane, looking at the wild things growing along the edges, I see snakeroot, white and lavender wild aster in profusion, wild bittersweet climbing a tall thorny tree (making it hard to collect), and boneset and wild hops. The sumac's lower leaves turn glorious red in early September, matching the berry horns that were bright red in late summer. Now the sumac berry horns have turned a rusty autumn red. Poison ivy climbs the trees and has turned a bright ruby color.

The harvest season is ending. The plants are turning inward now. Soon the lushness of the spring and early summer will be forgotten as the trees become bare and the ground turns brown from the fallen leaves.

It has been a good September in the garden, and there was time to sit in a chair on my front porch to enjoy it all. And now, I bid my September garden farewell.

IN THE KITCHEN IN SEPTEMBER

$\mathcal{I}$t is apple season here in the Midwest, and we are blessed with fresh apples. I can a few quarts of sliced apples and spices each September. When baking a quick pie or crisp, opening a jar is quick, easy and handy for wintertime use. September is when I prepare for the winter season ahead.

APPLE PIE

My mom sent me this recipe from two of her sisters; they made it for years. It is an old recipe originally coming from my maternal grandmother. It is delicious with ingredients already in the cupboard, but like all recipes, I "tweak" a little as noted at the end of the recipe.

256

3 c. apples, pared and sliced
3 T. sugar
1 tsp. cinnamon
Mix the apples, sugar and cinnamon together and put in bottom of greased 10" pie plate or an 8x8 pan.

In a bowl mix together:
1 stick butter (½ cup)
½ c. sugar
Dash salt
½ c. flour
1 tsp. baking powder
1 egg, beaten

Mix all and pour over apples. Bake at 350 degrees for 40 minutes. Note: If I have on hand, I may add 4 oz. cream cheese to the mixture.

OLD FASHIONED FRIED APPLES

This is a quick and easy comfort food.

For one person, wash and slice 1-2 apples, add to skillet with 1 T. butter or bacon drippings. Cover and cook until ALMOST done, then add a dash of cinnamon and 1 tsp. brown sugar or more and 1 T. chopped pecans.

For more servings, use 8 apples and when ALMOST done, add other adjusted ingredients. Good with ice cream.

APPLESAUCE

This is my process for making applesauce, which makes approximately 8 quarts of applesauce per bushel of apples.

Wash jars and apples. Chop apples into segments and put into a stainless steel pot to cook with ½ inch filtered tap water or organic apple juice. Put lid on and heat on medium high, watching so they don't scorch. If it gets dry on bottom, add a little more liquid, but the apples should be releasing their juices. Cook until apples seem soft (test with fork). I put a portion of cooked apples at a time through a hand mill/sieve. I use a Foley food mill purchased at a hardware store. (I do not use a food processor, as I do not want the seeds or skins). The sieve will separate the skins and seeds from the sauce. Return sieved apples back to the pan and turn heat down to very low. Keep hot until enough is made to fill the jars needed for the canner. (I do not season or sweeten the applesauce before canning. Sweetener such as maple syrup and cinnamon can be added at serving time).

Screw two-part lids on tightly. Fill the jars and process them in hot water bath for 20 minutes for pints and 25 minutes for quarts. The jars need to be covered with 1-inch water at boiling when starting the timing process. A pressure canner may be used instead. I find it wise to check out a canning manual for specific instructions before making anything that is canned.

Note: *The apple season lasts for two months in the Midwest with some varieties starting to ripen in August and some lasting into October.*

APPLE BUTTER
12 apples, washed and cut into fourths, skin and cores removed
1 ½ c. packed brown sugar
½ c. apple juice
1 T. lemon juice
1 T. cinnamon
1 tsp. ground allspice
1 tsp. ground nutmeg
½ tsp. ground cloves

Cook on medium heat in a stainless-steel pot with lid slightly ajar (I prefer to not use a crockpot). When soft, mash with masher or put in blender. Add sugar and spices and cook uncovered another hour or so, as this will let liquid escape and sauce will thicken. Watch so it does not scorch. When thickened, cool for 2 hours. Makes approximately 4 cups and can be kept in refrigerator for 3 weeks or process in water bath or pressure canner.

Note: *good varieties to use for Apple Butter are Gala, Honeycrisp and Braeburn*

APPLE CIDER MUFFINS (gluten free)

¼ c. sour cream or yogurt at room temperature
1/3 to 1/2 c. sugar (plus 2 T. for topping)
2 large eggs, room temperature, beaten
1/2 c. butter (1 stick) at room temp.
1 tsp. vanilla
¾ c. apple cider or apple juice at room temperature
1 ¾ c. gluten free flour (1-1 kind)
½ tsp. xanthan gum (if not already in GF flour)
1 ½ tsp. baking powder
¼ tsp. baking soda
1 tsp. cinnamon (plus 3/4 tsp. for topping)
Dash salt
1 apple, cored and thinly sliced (for topping)

Mix muffin ingredients together and fill muffin tins 3/4 full. Top each unbaked muffin with 3 thin apple slices. Mix together ¾ tsp. cinnamon + 2 T. sugar. Sprinkle on top of apples and bake 350 degrees for 20 minutes. Cool 10 minutes and serve. Makes 12-13 muffins.

IDEA: *CARAMEL APPLES ARE NEAT MADE WITH A SHORT BRANCH STUCK INTO them. Wash and dry the short branch first. I love this look in the autumn and what is better than a caramel apple? The caramel apple can be sprinkled with sea salt for even more flavor!*

AUTUMN EQUINOX

Ｔhe Autumn Equinox (Sept. 21-23) is the three-day period when the sun appears to stand still. Equinox means *equal*, and the day and night are each 12 hours long. The sun will rise in the true east and set in the true west. It is a time to begin once again to find my balance in life as the seasons change. From this time forward, all of life begins to turn inward.

The Equinox marks what is considered the mid-point of autumn, as many say autumn begins August 1st and ends Oct. 31st. For farming ancestors of long ago, the fall equinox and throughout the following month was the last harvest of the year. At the end of gathering, storing the harvest away, and preparing for the upcoming winter, the people had time and good reason to celebrate with plentiful foods, feasting and dancing. I set aside time to honor the seasons and be grateful for what each season offers, especially the bountiful harvests and the blessings of Mother Earth.

There is harmony in autumn, and a luster in its sky,
which through the summer is not heard or seen,
as if it could not be, as it if had not been.
–Percy Bysshe Shelley (1792-1822)

FAIRY RING

The fairy ring beyond the garden is mysterious looking in the daylight, and under the full moon it is magical. For the fairies, it must be a delightful place to live. The fairy ring is a circle of a dozen or more big mushrooms, some as big as a dinner plate, dressed in a soft white color. I feel blessed to see this gift of Nature, as fairy rings are not spotted often. The name *fairy ring* is a loving name given to this mushroom phenomenon when it appears overnight as if by magic, and disappearing nearly as quickly.

BROOM CORN

*B*room corn is not really a corn at all. It is more of a tall grass that forms a beautiful fan-shaped seed head. This grass is actually used in making brooms and is better known as *millet* or *shatter cane*. It is cultivated the same way as oats or barley in northern Europe, as the seeds are small and round.

I have seen it used in birdseed, and it is easy to grow by sprinkling the seed from a head into the garden or a place I want it to grow. It is a sun-loving annual, and can grow eight feet tall, so it needs an area that can handle it. The seed can be ordered from nursery catalogs. When ready to harvest, I cut it off in the length desired and hang upside down to dry. I have found that mice love it as much as the birds. I set it into an arrangement in a big jug in a corner, and it will last a long time, but does shed seeds as it dries. If the seeds are allowed to be eaten off by birds or mice outside, the picked-off fan shapes that are left can be bundled to make a broom. It can also be dried, and the seeds will drop if tapped gently. The plant is extensively cultivated in America for the manufacture of brooms and brushes. Brooms have been used for centuries to sweep the floor, however most brooms today are made of plastic.

Benjamin Franklin is recognized as introducing broom corn to the United States in the early 1700's. Before 1800, brooms in America were handmade. Cooking was much different, as stoves had not been invented yet. Cooking was done outside over an open fire or in a huge fireplace in the kitchen. Reflector ovens were also used. Fire had to be well tended. A broom was an important tool in keeping the hearth clean. Unfortunately, really good brooms did not exist, and dust and ashes were a part of life.

Broom corn yields a white flour which can be used for making bread, and the grain is used for feeding cattle, horses and poultry. The grain is diuretic (stimulates urination) and demulcent (soothes mucus membranes) if taken as a decoction.

To grow broom corn, scatter a few seeds in the spring or let them fall in the autumn, and have broom corn for the birds or for décor inside or to make a handmade broom!

GOLDENROD

❦

oldenrod is a native plant where I live in the Midwest, and it is Nebraska's state flower. It has been mistakenly maligned as causing hay fever in the fall. Since it blooms brightly at the same time as subtle green-flowering ragweed, many have thought goldenrod was the sneeze-causing culprit, but it is not – and it is actually a wonderful plant.

There are many varieties of goldenrod, and they bloom at different times throughout the autumn season. Where I live it begins to bloom the first of August, and some varieties will bloom through all of September. Besides being a beautiful and cheerful plant, it was also revered by the early settlers and Native Americans for its medicine. I gather goldenrod each autumn to use in making my herbal remedies also.

When I pick a bouquet of goldenrod for my table, I gather it before it is in full bloom and sit it in a vase to dry without water. If it is picked too late after coming into full bloom, the flower head will turn into fluff within a day. After all, the goal of plants is to make seed and reproduce.

Goldenrod is a helpful plant I tincture and infuse in oil. I use the just-opened blossoms as well as leaves and use the fresh plant for tincture. When infusing in oil, I make sure it is dried first, otherwise my oil infusion could mold. Goldenrod was traditionally used for arthritis, allergies, asthma, fatigue, and urinary tract health. I use it for all of those as well. Research is now finding that Goldenrod tones the urinary tract and helps detoxify the kidneys. It has been used for UTIs, kidney stones, and incontinence.

Goldenrod is the base of the arthritis salve I make and use. It is a gift of Mother Earth and is one of my favorite medicinal herbs, and it never ceases to amaze me how many of our wild plants will heal our bodies as well as our spirits.

September

The goldenrod is yellow;
The corn is turning brown;
The trees in apple orchards with fruit are bending down.
The gentian's bluest fringes are curling in the sun;
In dusty pods, the milkweed hidden silk has spun.
The sedges flaunt their harvest, in every meadow nook;
And asters by the brook-side make asters in the brook.
From dewy lanes at morning, the grapes' sweet odor rise;
At noon, the roads all flutter with yellow butterflies.
By all these lovely tokens
September days are here,
With summer's best weather,
And autumn's best of cheer.
-Helen Hunt Jackson (1830-1885)

ACORNS

It is autumn, and like the leaves, the acorns also let go and plummet to the earth below. Acorns are the sweet little seedpod of the oak tree. The acorn is food for the little creatures to store away for winter, and when the squirrels forget where they buried an acorn, then the acorn grows into a tree. I gather a few acorns each autumn as an autumn ritual. I love the acorns and find it interesting that the settlers and Native Americans ground the acorn nut into a flour to use. In the last few years I have started a small collection of acorn items, including a wool acorn "pinkeep" made by a friend, an acorn candy container from another friend, and several actual acorns. I especially love the big fuzzy caps of the acorns from the Bur Oak tree. Acorns represent life and new beginnings.

"Little by little," the acorn said,
as it slowly sank in its mossy bed,
"I am improving every day, hidden deep in the earth away."
Little by little it sipped the dew,
downward it sent out a threadlike root,
upon the top sprung a tiny shoot.

Day after day, and year after year,
Little by little the leaves appear;
And the slender branches spread far and wide,
Until the mighty oak is the forest's pride.
(Author unknown)

OSAGE ORANGE TREE

❧

The sky is falling, the sky is falling!

No, it is another green hedge ball falling from the tree above. The Osage orange tree is dropping its fruit now. The fruits are also called hedge balls, hedge apples or horse apples. I am picking them up off the drive, my walking path and from the flowerbeds. Most are the size of apples or oranges, but a few are the size of huge grapefruits, so one does not want to be standing under an Osage tree this time of year – especially if there is wind. The chartreuse green makes them easy to see, and with their pebbly surface they are a decorator's delight, even if only for a few days. I put them in a wooden bowl with sprigs of fresh bittersweet, and I love the way it looks. I watch the hedge balls daily in the bowl, as they will turn brown and rot within the week. I enjoy them for a few days and then replace with a few fresh hedge apples.

Growing up we had a row of hedge apple trees separating the field from the road. My woods today are interspersed with them, as they are a native and invasive. The squirrels will eat hedge apples if they cannot find anything else to eat, but my dad always said the horses and cows do not eat them. There is an old myth that placing them in cellars or basements will keep spiders and insects away, but that has been proven untrue. In an old cellar I would give it a try anyway.

The Osage orange tree was used in pioneer days to make fences across the Midwest by planting many trees. It is said to be *the tree that tamed the West*. It is dense-growing with long thorns, so the fence kept everything in or out. Fence posts made of the hard wood of the Osage orange will last 100 years or more, as termites will not eat it. The roots are covered in an orange bark. I love this beautiful wood and the endurance of this survivalist tree, and I have more than a few that live in my woods.

The Osage tree is letting go of its fruit around my yard and down my lane. Autumn is about letting go like the seeds, fruits and leaves do; pulling in and going deeper, as the roots take nutrients down with them as they ready themselves for the next season.

October

THE VIEW FROM MY WINDOW

There is no season
when such pleasant and sunny spots may be lighted on,
and produces so pleasant an effect on the feelings,
as now in October.
–Nathaniel Hawthorne

*F*are thee well, summer days – I bid you goodbye until next year.

I am ready to welcome October. I open the windows for the autumn breezes to flow through, savoring the mild days, readying myself for the briskness of the next season to come.

The early morning was too cool to sit on the big front porch and sip my cup of hot tea as I would have loved to do. Early mornings are the best part of my day when everything is fresh and renewed, including me. Those sweet and magical early hours do not last long, and then the day begins all over again.

Autumn is definitely here with cooler nights and warm days. I wish autumn days would last forever, or at least three months at a stretch. But autumn in the Midwest is fleeting, and I cherish each day. Sometimes it all changes quickly, from the heat of summer right into the cold last part of autumn. I want to savor every smell, sound, taste and sight of this glorious month. The first leaves start twirling to the earth. I pick a last small bouquet of wild asters to enjoy on my kitchen table and a few more chartreuse green hedge apples have dropped in my lane. The dense and shady woods will soon be sparse and twiggy with the branches and vines denuded of their summer cloak of greenery. Old bird nests will be easier to see without their leafy camouflage, and a lone deer can be seen sauntering slowly through the trees. I soak up every bit of the autumn days, knowing the next colder season will soon be here.

By mid-October in the Midwest, the proverbial frost is on the pumpkin – almost. With global warming, the frost holds off a little longer, now waiting until late in the month close to Halloween. Mother Nature gives us her fair warning that the days and nights are changing. Big orange pumpkins are at the markets, tree leaves are turning colors and the crickets are chirping. Soon wood smoke will fill the air, vines of bright orange wild bittersweet will cling to the fencerows to use for decoration in my home, and there will be hot apple cider to enjoy at the end of my day.

October afternoons are a perfect time to be outside. I carry my old basket with me wherever I go to put a few treasures in that I might find as I wander here and yonder doing my autumn chores. I clip the rose hips, add some crabapples to my stash, and a few pretty seed heads, leaving most of the pods and seed heads for the birds as food this winter. The white marigolds planted amongst the tomatoes are now drying up their flower heads and making seeds, so I clip a few to plant next spring. The needle-like leaves of lavender smell as wonderful as the flower when it blooms, so I snip a few stalks to add to a sleep pillow for sweet dreams. And before I go back inside I will cut a few small branches of the rosemary bush to make mini herb wreaths for the soup pot this winter. Rosemary is considered an annual here in the Midwest, but in Kansas on the south side of the house it winters over, as long as the cold is not too harsh or prolonged.

I gather seeds, feeling a bit like Johnny Appleseed, and toss them into the wildflower area, hoping more Queen Anne's lace and wild indigo will take hold in the earth and grow.

I live in a woodsy area with many trees, and there is always something to love about a tree, whether the leaves are bright summer green or beginning to turn golden yellow with autumn days. Because of lack of rain, leaves are falling earlier this year, and the stark bare outline of the trees are very noticeable. Each tree has its own personality, color and characteristics. Soon it will not be the leaves that we notice, or the color of the leaves, but the bark and branches of the trees.

As October ends, most of the branches are bare,
we can see more sky.
– Gladys Taber

The colors of autumn amaze me year after year. I am enthralled as I drive down a city street with the overhanging branches of colorful trees, and many times I stop to take it all in.

Everyone must take time to sit still and watch the leaves turn.
–Elizabeth Lawrence

275

I pick up leaves to press, which is an autumnal ritual year after year. I watch the shimmering leaves gently tumbling down to the earth, until a breeze comes along, and then they swirl around me before they pile up in the corners. Their ultimate goal is to make a connection with Mother Earth. And on the earth they will stay, creating a carpet of gold, yellow, red and then brown, as they nourish the earth, enriching the soil for the plants to grow.

Every leaf speaks bliss to me, fluttering from the autumn tree.
-Emily Jane Bronte

The early autumn rains have brought an end to summer and a richness to the colors of the autumn earth. Even the most common weeds are beautiful. Everything is more vivid, and I am aware of the individuality of each stalk and stem and seed and weed. I feel the need to absorb the richness of October days to their complete fullness.

Foggy October mornings are a favorite time to take an early walk. Even on a gray and dreary morning, there is much to appreciate in this most wonderful month.

I saw Old Autumn in the misty morn stand,
shadowless like silence, listening to silence.
–Thomas Hood

After my walk, I sit at my desk looking out the big window. I am watching a grey squirrel playing a game of hide-and-seek around the brilliant red oak tree in my yard. She is scampering here and there, and I am sure there is a little play involved as she sees me watching her, but mainly she is putting the little acorns away for her winter meals.

From little acorns mighty oaks do grow.
-American proverb

Acorns are covering the ground from the oak trees. I never tire of visiting the big grandmother Bur Oak tree by the lake where I like to collect a bowl full of the big acorns with their bristly caps. I will admire these acorns for a month or two and then put them out for the squirrels as a winter treat.

The creation of a thousand forests is in one acorn.
–Ralph Waldo Emerson

On my morning walks, I stop and hug the trees and thank them for *being*. I collect the colorful leaves and press them in a big book when I get back to my house and eventually will add the dried pressed leaves to the front of a notecard. The oranges, reds and yellows are becoming vibrant now as October progresses.

October's poplars are flaming torches
lighting the way to winter.
–Nova Bair

The haunting cry of Canadian geese breaks the silence as they fly overhead, migrating their way across the sky. I look forward to hearing their *honking* and *squawking* as I bid them farewell until their next trip. It is a ritual to stop and watch their "V" formation flying above me as they circle and settle down on the watershed lake nearby. Their familiar sound never fails to stir the wildness in me. Because of global warming, the geese sometimes winter here after they find a good spot to call home for a few months or more.

The owls have begun their *who-who* hooting again after being fairly quiet during the summer months. They communicate back and forth while searching for their mates and hunting their next meal. This is another of nature's sounds I love to hear.

I am grateful to live in the Midwest where we experience distinct seasons of the year, and I am thankful for the beauty and energy each season brings. Pictures cannot capture the true beauty of October, and a snapshot only serves as a reminder of how colorful the month is. I have always loved taking pictures, composing vignettes through the lens, or finding the perfect feature to snap. But for almost five years during a difficult time in my life, the camera laid quietly on a shelf. Now I have picked it up once again as the autumn sunshine beckons me to take a few snapshots outside. I want to remember the golden beauty of the creek south of my log cabin home. The trees are mainly golds and yellows, like a sunburst on the horizon, and I want it to stay this way, but I know the leaves will soon be gone as they are drifting down on my shoulders as I take pictures. I want this view to last forever.

The autumn air is filled with cricket songs, and I believe they are warning of a chill coming tomorrow. I have clipped bittersweet from my tame vines in the backyard, which produce faithfully each year. My long farm table is a harvest scene with the bittersweet, little pumpkins and a few gourds decorating it this season. The wild bittersweet is the prettiest and showiest of all, with brighter burnt orange and larger berries, but it is being called an invasive weed in some states now, so is being eradicated to my dismay. It is hard to wrap my mind around that idea, as bittersweet mainly grows in fencerows and to the top of locust or Osage orange trees, and the birds enjoy the beautiful berries in winter. Not long ago, wild bittersweet was quite prevalent, but it only grew in the woods and not fields. It lends that special autumn touch to my decorating, but now I find it rare to see a wild bunch even at a Farmers' Market. It saddens my heart. I have tried growing it from wild seed, but cannot get it to grow, so wild bittersweet may be but an elusive memory one day. Now I settle for the tame I grow, but it is not the same.

The heart and soul is inspired by the simple gifts of nature.
-unknown

Feeling the forces of the season, I gathered the last stalks of goldenrod to put in a vase, along with a few small bunches of bright autumn leaves, making a pretty autumn bouquet. I remember to hang corn in a symbolic tribute to the harvest season and to honor Mother Earth. On my front door I made a hanger of three dried hard-shell elongated gourds. I strung a garland of smaller gourds to hang across the fireplace. I enjoy gourds of all kinds, from the tiny dancing gourds to the larger bushel gourds – all are marvels of nature.

After growing the gourds, they are harvested and stored in a place where they will not freeze while they continue to dry (up to a year) and the outer skin develops mold. It is this mold that creates the beautiful mottling on the hard shell. Once the mold has formed and the gourd has dried out, I scrub the mold off. There are no two that look alike because of the varied patterns the mold created. I have always been fascinated and drawn to growing and collecting gourds.

I'm so glad I live in a world where there are Octobers.
– L.M. Montgomery (Anne of Green Gables)

My big three-foot-long antique *make-do* trencher, with repairs of tin on both ends, is filled full with dried smooth-skinned gourds of all sizes, a few mini white and orange pumpkins, some broom corn stuck in for added texture, and a vine of bittersweet. In the middle of all this autumn natural décor sits a quart-size jar candle (elevated by a block of wood) for a perfect harvest vignette. This long old trencher sits atop a seven-foot-wide, thirty-drawer chest that I fondly call *my apothecary,* but in reality it was probably used for tools. It stands forty-two inches tall, and each drawer is about twelve-by-twelve inches, making it a unique storage and décor piece.

The shocks of corn, pumpkins and mums are standing guard at the entrance to the long covered front porch of my home. While at the store I could not pass up the large blooming rust-colored mum plants, and after they have done their duty as décor on my front porch, I will cut them down and find a permanent spot for them planted along the garden fence. My front porch tells everyone *it is October.*

The beauty that shimmers in the yellow afternoons –
October, who could ever clutch it?
– Ralph Waldo Emerson

Now the garden is ready to be put to bed for its long winter's rest, and I have picked the last of the tomatoes and peppers. The black killer frost will happen soon. October is a reminder of cider, wood smoke, making soup, and digging the roots of dandelion and burdock. Today I am thinking about apple crisp and caramel apples. Apple butter and applesauce have been made and stored on the pantry shelves. Harvesting one's own crop of apples is a special joy in the autumn. I am looking forward to a trip to Farmer's Market or an orchard nearby, and there I will buy a pumpkin or two for the front porch, as well as apples and apple cider.

"This is my favorite month of the year!" I hear this refrain often from friends in the month of October, and I heartily agree. I think of wooly sweaters, hot chocolate, sitting by the fireplace with a roaring fire, pulling in and reading a good book or knitting a neck scarf and enjoying the first crisp and cool days that October brings.

> *October is the month*
> *When the smallest breeze*
> *Gives us a shower of autumn leaves.*
> *Bonfires and pumpkins*
> *Leaves sailing down –*
> *October is red and golden and brown.*
> – Can Teach Songs

October is about the Harvest moon, the *Maple Leaf Festival* in our little village close by, making pumpkin muffins, putting the gourds in a basket under the coffee table, taking a picture of the mounds of mums blooming profusely, preparing for Halloween and the grandsons' anticipation of a night of trick-or-treating and the meaning of the day, and getting the houseplants back into the house before it is too cold for them outside.

I think of cinnamon and cloves, chili soup, planting a few more spring flowering bulbs before the ground freezes and walking barefoot in the grass, absorbing some last minute *earthing* energy before snow is on the ground. I need to gather some wild grapevines to put across the fireplace mantel this autumn along with a few berried vines. And my family and I will take a short country drive to *Signal Oak Hill,* as it is an autumn ritual for us. The bluff is historical as well as an impressive overlook for the entire valley below and the town of Lawrence, Kansas. Pictures are always taken along the old fence with the valley below, and from the pictures I see how the grandsons have grown each year. One day they may bring their children to this same spot as an autumn tradition and ritual.

The first whiff of wood smoke is in the air. The autumn chill comes in the morning and then again in the evening. I am thinking as I bend down now and then to pick up another acorn or another pretty leaf, that I will light a candle or start a fire in the fireplace this evening. The sight and smell of the first crackling fire of the season comforts my soul and takes me back to another time when our ancestors did the same. Firewood is another of the woodland's riches that comes to mind in the autumn of the year. When the air gets cold outside, a crackling fire epitomizes hearth and home. There is a sense of security in having a neatly stacked woodpile handy by the back door.

The trees are many and varied where I live close to the Vinland Valley. It is on the western edge of the eastern hardwood forests, with many oaks and maples, plus sycamore, bur oaks, and elms, but the oaks and maples are the ones we notice most of all in the autumn when their rich colors are vividly bright. I see many city folk this time of year driving along the country roads and around the county lake, filling their senses with the colors and scenes of autumn.

The summer clothes are put away and the sweaters are unpacked from storage to warm me on the chilly days ahead. October is a month I call a *comfort* month – a month of warming up, getting cozy inside my home and thinking about hot chocolate nights and hearty soup days.

> *The leaves fall, the wind blows,*
> *and the farm country slowly changes*
> *from the summer cottons into its winter wools.*
> -Henry Beston

In October, the weather and nature changes from day to day. It is a reminder of darker days coming, of pulling into ourselves and finding our balance again on this earth. I am grateful for food on my table from the harvest, a warm hearth, and the beauty of October days.

THE FULL MOON IN OCTOBER

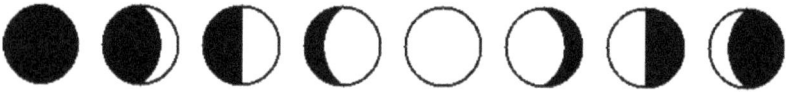

Many paths lead from the foot of the mountain,
But at the Peak we all gaze at the sky
and the same bright moon.
-Ikkyu

ountry lore tells us that if by the time of a full moon in October there has been no frost, we will have no frost until the full moon of November. This was "grassroots" weather forecasting by our ancestors. It is the month of the *Harvest Moon,* the *Wolf Moon,* the *Hunters Moon, Falling Leaf Moon,* and *Frost on the Grass Moon.* At the peak of the harvest, farmers can work late into the night by the light of the full moon. The October moon is especially magical and bewitching as it appears full and orange in the darkened sky. The moon looks bigger in the fall than any other time of year. Perhaps it is just the crisp nights and darkness of the countryside that makes it appear fuller. It pleases my soul to stand outside and gaze at the October moon or dance and sing to her. It is a simple October pleasure.

The October full moon sometimes occurs right before Halloween. Then the little *tricksters* have extra light to guide their paths on this moody and mysterious night.

When witches go riding,
And black cats are seen,
The moon laughs and whispers,
'Tis near Halloween.
- unknown

IN THE GARDEN IN OCTOBER

HERB SOUP WREATHS

*T*he soup wreaths I make are simple to add to the soup pot. I put together the herbs I want to add to a vegetable or chicken soup this way: I take one eight-inch sprig of rosemary or chive leaf and tie the ends together with cotton string or heavier quilting thread, leaving longer ends on both pieces. I add sprigs of thyme to the left and one very small sprig of sage to the right and tie those to the herb wreath, adding sprigs of chives. Rosemary can be strong tasting, so another way is to tie a small bunch of herbs together, beginning with several sprigs of thyme, adding a leaf of sage, a very small twig of rosemary, and some chive leaves like a little bouquet.

An herb wreath is simple to make and pretty. The following day it will start to dry. I make several to dry and have handy to add to my soups during the upcoming winter season. I put the dried wreath in the simmering soup pot the last 15 to 30 minutes of cooking and remove before serving. If using rosemary, I remember it is a strong-tasting herb, and a little goes a long way. I add extra thyme

286

to my wreath for my chicken soup or make smaller thyme soup wreaths using only the thyme. Once well dried, I store the soup wreaths or clusters in a tin box or a wide-mouthed jar. I will use throughout the winter in my chicken or vegetable soups, or corn chowder soup. I also like to tie these to a package at the holidays or for gift giving.

AUTUMN POTPOURRI

1 c. dried sage leaves

2 c. dried goldenrod blossoms and leaves

1 c. dried celery leaves

½ c. sunflower seeds

½ c. pumpkin seeds

1 c. pods, like rose hips, indigo, etc.

1 c. colorful corn, shelled

2 c. small acorns from pin oak tree

1 c. tiny pinecones from nature/or craft store

This is a great way to use end-of-season items — change, omit or add to ingredients. Potpourri is pretty in a glass bowl or container, but it usually ends up in one of my old wooden bowls. When the autumn season is over, I throw it outside. The leaves will blow away and the birds and squirrels will enjoy the treat.

GARLIC

By the end of October my garlic is planted for the next year. The first time I planted my garlic this way it seemed wrong to me, and I feared it might not make it through the winter. The autumn-planted garlic is easy to do. Once planted, I forget about it and next spring little green plants appear earlier than anything else in my garden, to my heart's delight.

I plant organic individual cloves, breaking them away from the mother bulb, leaving the bits of paper covering on each clove as protection. They are planted three inches deep and four-to-six inches apart, pointed end up. After planting I water lightly. In a week or two I cover with dry straw and forget about them. They will grow a few inches yet in the autumn as long as weather is mild, and when winter comes the snow will cover them. If there is no snow, the straw will keep them snug. In the early spring I take the straw off and let them grow. They will be ready to harvest early July or any time after. I find the harvested garlic does not store well for me, so after curing it I ferment or pickle the garlic, or I use from the garden as needed, leaving the rest growing underground a little longer.

It is said that garlic is very good for the immune system. The Native Americans believed it to be good for kidney functions and kidney stones also.

> *It never really stops, this business of growing things –*
> *garlic goes into the ground in October,*
> *just as other frost-killed crops*
> *are getting piled onto the compost heap.*
> *Food is not a product but a process, and it never sleeps.*
> *It just goes underground for awhile.*
> From *Animal, Vegetable, Miracle* by Barbara Kingsolver

IN THE KITCHEN IN OCTOBER

Thyme is the blending herb — it pulls flavors together.

AUTUMN HERB CHICKEN SOUP
2 ½ qt. chicken broth
2 to 4 cooked chicken breasts, shredded
1 stalk celery, finely diced
1/2 c. onion, finely diced
2 carrots, peeled and sliced
1/4 tsp. turmeric
Salt and pepper to taste
2 tsp. All-Purpose Herb Mix (see January)
1/4 c. brown rice, rinsed (or leftover rice), optional. Can use 1 c. cooked rice from freezer
Herb wreath optional, if using, add last 15-20 minutes and then remove.

Put all in soup pot. Cook 45 minutes to one hour until rice and carrots are done.

PARMESAN CORN BREAD
2 c. self-rising corn meal mix
1 egg, beaten
1/8 c. oil or melted butter
1 ¾ c. buttermilk
1 to 2 tsp. All-Purpose Herb Mix (see January)
1/4 c. Parmesan cheese, shredded for topping after baked

Mix all ingredients together and put in greased 8"x8" pan. Bake
25-30 min. at 350 degrees. Sprinkle cheese on top of bread after
removing from oven. Serve with soup.
Note: *The gluten-free cornbread mix from health food store is very good.
Add the herbs and cheese to it.*

PUMPKIN CRUNCH CAKE
20 oz. canned pumpkin puree
1 can (12 oz.) evaporated milk
3 eggs
3/4 c. sugar
3 tsp. cinnamon
Topping:
1 box yellow cake mix, regular or gluten free
1 c. chopped pecans
3/4 c. butter, melted

Mix all except cake mix, pecans and butter and put in 9x13 greased
pan. Sprinkle dry cake mix over top of pumpkin mix. Sprinkle
pecans over top of cake mix, drizzle with melted butter. Bake 50
minutes at 350 degrees.

NIGHT OF THE WITCHES

*I*n the witch's garden in October the mugwort, lavender, rosemary and mint still grow until a hard freeze makes them go underground.

And what do witches have to do with gardens, herbs and flowers?

I enjoy my plants, wild and tame, and the process of making my medicines from them as my ancestors did before me. *All Hallows Eve* is a time to honor those who lived before us. The witches were the helpers, healers and midwives who often lived on the edge of the woods and were feared by the village people. They grew herb gardens, searched out the wild herbs in the woods, and made medicines to give to the villagers. These "witches" helped birth the babies and were present when someone died and transitioned. Their *witch-craft* was the craft of making medicines from the plants. Their *incantation* was the intention of prayer and blessing for healing.

I put on a witch's hat and a black shawl each *All Hallows Eve* to honor the ancestral witches. I think of them often when I make my tincture medicines and lotions and potions, salves and balms. I think how they were persecuted if a healing failed, or someone looked at another for too long, and an accusation was made. The wise old women were exterminated. This is woman's history. Many villages were left with no one to do the healing, and valuable traditions and oral herbal wisdom was lost. Halloween, *All Hallows Eve*, is a time of reflection. I wonder if the world has changed?

On *Samhain*, the predecessor of our Halloween day, it is a good time to read the history of the witches. Learning about the witches and who they were is important history for everyone to know and never forget.

In the witch's garden, the gate is open wide.
"Come inside," says the witch,
"Dears, do come inside.
No flowers in my garden.
Nothing minty, nothing chivey.
Come inside, come inside, see my poison ivy."
-Lillian Moore (1909-2004)

OCTOBER NATURE PROJECTS

❦

PRESSED LEAVES

Preserving leaves is easy and fun to do in October. Collect pretty, brightly colored leaves. Cut squares of wax paper to cover the leaves, putting the leaf between two pieces of wax paper, sandwich style. Place an old washcloth open on the ironing board or use a towel on the counter. Put the leaf and wax paper "sandwich" on the cloth, lay another open washcloth on top (to keep iron clean from wax on paper) and press medium heat (no steam) until adhered together. Allow to cool.

One way to use these is to cut around the leaf, leaving a small margin of wax paper, which holds everything together. Punch a hole through all, or use a needle and thread to string the leaves, making a garland for the window. Another way to use them is to peel away the wax paper. The wax, ironed onto the leaf, will preserve the leaf for the remainder of the season. These are pretty to use on a plate or table for decoration.

Note: *If doing this with children, adult supervision is needed.*

GHOSTS

Collect locust pods that fall from the tree. They will be elongated, flat and brown. With a small bottle of white acrylic craft paint, cover both sides of the pod once or twice. With a tiny brush, paint on an oval mouth and two round eyes — or the eyes could be glued-on "google eyes" from craft store. With needle and white thread, string through the top to hang on a branch or as a garland. I like to use quilters thread, as it is heavier. Regular thread, doubled, will work.

JACK – O -LANTERNS

The locust tree pod ghosts and these jack-o-lanterns go well hung together on a small tree branch that is stuck into a jar of sand. We call it a Halloween tree.

The jack-o-lanterns are made from wild milkweed pods found along the roadside or in the meadow. Be sure all the silky seeds inside have dispersed into the wild. With a small bottle of orange acrylic craft paint, paint both sides of the milkweed pod. One side is a little bumpy, but a foam brush will cover it well. When the paint is dry, use black paint or marker to make the triangle eyes, triangle nose, and a curved full mouth. When dry, I take a dab of white paint on a tiny pointed brush or toothpick and put a slender line of white on the right side only of the black eyes. With needle and thread, string through the top and make a hanger. Hang these on a Halloween tree (branch) or a garland.

A simple and inexpensive gift of nature.

November

THE VIEW THROUGH MY WINDOW

Come ye thankful people come
Raise the song of Harvest home,
All is safely gathered in, Ere the winter storms begin
– Alford

The first light snow has come and gone, giving a sense of the winter coming. The autumn leaves are gathering on the path, crunching as I walk on them. When they are swept and gathered they will be added to the garden as mulch or left in place where they fall to go back into the earth, replenishing it.

I wrap up in my soft woolen sweater to ward away the morning November chill – a reminder of the many rich textures in this season. I look out the window at the layers created by earth, hills and trees. The garden perennials, trees, shrubs and all the little living creatures are preparing for the days ahead, as I am. Many are already slumbering in their long winter's nap. I am anxious to sit by the hearth of a warm fire today, sipping hot herbal tea and reading a good book. November is beckoning me. It is in our ancestral DNA to take it slow now, to pull inside into hearth and home, and to hibernate like the other creatures.

We have entered the season of darkness – a time for introspectiveness, looking inward, burrowing in, and cocooning. I would like to stay in my warm bed on this chilly morning, but instead I sit up, wondering what has awakened me at this early hour – it is still quite dark outside. I never set an alarm, but rely on my inner clock to tell me when to wake up, and it is usually early. The clock reads 5:00 a.m., and still I am wondering why I am wide-awake. I reach for my robe and go to the living room to sit in my big old chair and listen... and then I hear them. Owls hooting. This is common in my neck of the woods. It is the *call of the wild* or *call IN the wild,* and I listen to them conversing with their mates or a neighboring owl as they serenade me for almost an hour while I contemplate my day ahead.

We were blessed with the bounty of Mother Earth during the summer and fall months, and the pantry is well stocked for the winter months ahead. Farmers' Market is nearly over for the season. It is a mad rush as people show up on the final day to purchase the last of the squash, fresh eggs, meat and other items not grown in our gardens this year. I keep a good supply of squash and sweet potatoes in the pantry ready for baking in the oven, as it is simple food to fix and delicious to eat, and the smells coming from a warm oven are most inviting this time year.

In the month of November, I am reminded again that I am a *gatherer* in life. My knitting basket sits close by my big chair now and holds knitting and wool appliqué projects. I gather my favorite things around me. Living in the woods, with the prairie meadows close by, there is much to gather on a warmer-than-normal November day. Taking a short walk, I clip the poppy seed pods from my garden edge, and on the prairie I find more wild indigo seed stems with many pods still full of seeds that rattle inside. I leave behind many seeds to fall to the ground over the winter to grow another year.

Walking a little further, I find milkweed pods and clip the long stems. The silky seeds have long since blown away to scatter here and yonder. I will put the wild grasses, stems of pods, burgundy sumac heads and rose hip stems into a tall crock in a corner of the front porch. I leave the sunflower and black-eyed Susan stems in the meadow for the birds to enjoy when the snow falls later on.

The *Artemisia* (wild sage) and garden sage were picked at the first of the month and put into a big basket and placed on top of an old painted blue cupboard. I clip a few more of the beige dried hydrangea flowers and add them to the *Artemisia* and sage basket. I love this neutral-colored bouquet from Mother Earth. The simple pleasures that await me when I take a short walk on a nice November day make my heart and soul sing.

November is the month of gratitude, a time we give thanks for our family, friends, food and shelter. I am grateful this day was set aside in 1863 by Abraham Lincoln for families to come together in celebration of the bounty and beauty of the natural world, the warmth of home and hearth, family and friends, and the tradition of sharing everything that makes life meaningful. We offer our thanks for the earth's abundance this time of year and all year through.

Thanksgiving Day comes, by statute, once a year.
To the honest man it comes as frequently
as the heart of gratitude will allow.
-Edward Sanford Martin

A large papier-mâché turkey, a gift from a friend, sits on the table in the entry as a symbol of Thanksgiving and the month of November. A wreath made of autumn leaves hangs above it, setting the tone of this autumnal holiday for all who cross the threshold of my home in the woods. The centerpiece for the long farm table is made of small branches, five white votive candles in holders, a few Clementine oranges, corn kernels sprinkled around and dried colorful leaves scattered throughout – it says *Autumn* at first glance. It is a reminder of the harvest feasts held long ago. The family clasps hands, and each person says what they are most grateful for with the words spoken most often being *the love for family*. It is Thanksgiving, and I am thankful for so much.

Give Thanks
For the hay and the corn and the wheat that is reaped,
For the labor well done, and the barns that are heaped,
For the sun and the dew and the sweet honeycomb,
For the rose and the song and the harvest brought home —
Thanksgiving!
For the trade and the skill and the wealth in our land,
For the cunning and strength of the workingman's hand,
For the good that our artists and poets have taught,
For the friendship that hope and affection have brought —
Thanksgiving!
For the homes that with purest affection are blest,
For the season of plenty and well-deserved rest,
For the country extending from sea unto sea;
For land that is known as the "Land of the Free" —
Thanksgiving!
-author unknown

The house smells comforting and warm this time of year, doors and windows are closed tightly against the chilly wind, and from the oven drifts the aroma of fruitcake baking for two hours at low temperature. Today, soup will be the mainstay food, made with nourishing homemade broth from the leftover locally raised free-range turkey we had for Thanksgiving dinner. The skin is used as well as bones, simmering to pull all the nutrients into the broth, then freezing it for a nutritious base for any soup. Making broth is simple and easy, as well as being good for body and soul.

A few of my favorite blessings in November:
- Autumn sights and scents
- Lighted candles
- Fire burning warmly and brightly in the fireplace
- Thanksgiving Day with family
- Pumpkins and gourds of all kinds
- Wild turkeys in the meadow
- Fruitcake made and topped with rum sauce to enjoy at Christmas
- Herbs made into winter medicine
- Potpourri simmering on the stove
- Homespun yarn knitted into a scarf to give as a gift
- Homemade soups

I saved seeds from the Halloween pumpkins. Pumpkin seeds are one of nature's almost perfect foods. They can be roasted whole or the hulled seeds (the heart) can be purchased at health food stores. The pumpkin seeds are full of vitamins and minerals. Traditional medicinal uses were for treating prostrate and bladder problems, but have also been known to help with depression. The seeds have been used for years by Native Americans for kidney problems and the elimination of intestinal parasites. Pumpkin seeds are traditionally recommended in some countries as "brain food." Other studies have shown they prevent hardening of the arteries and help regulate cholesterol levels. Pumpkin seeds are a gift from Mother Earth.

In November, if there is any good left of the Halloween pumpkins, I will cut it in one-by-one-inch chunks and roll the chunks in a cinnamon and cloves mixture, and then string the chunks to dry across the fireplace. I love the way it looks and smells.

Things to do in November:

- Fill the window boxes with pumpkins, gourds, corn and berries
- Collect seed from dried flowers in the garden
- Bake pumpkin bread
- Make spiced apple cider using mulling spices
- Make my special blend of simmering spices
- Take a walk in the woods to feel the crunch of leaves underfoot
- Gather old vines from the wild honeysuckle or wild grape to make a wreath for the front door or lay on the fireplace mantle
- Most of all, enjoy the month of November and give thanks

A few days ago, I walked along the edge of the lake and was treated to the crunch and rustle of leaves with each step I made. The acoustics of this season are different and all sounds, no matter how hushed, are as crisp as the autumn air.
–Eric Sloane

In November, I start to feed the birds at the bird feeders. They are happy for the food and a joy to observe from my big kitchen-dining window. The goldfinches are beginning to show a change in their feather color, fading from bright yellow to yellow-brown. They still feed on the foxtail near the edge of the woods. The downy woodpecker is fun to watch, as are the flickers hanging onto the side of the suet feeder. The cardinals enjoy the seed at dusk. I now eat my evening meal at the window, timing it just right as the birds fly in to feed, providing entertainment as I observe them.

And now that it is evening, I finish the inside chores needing done and get ready to find a good book to read before I go to bed early, as hibernation is calling to me. It is November.

November comes and November goes,
With the last red berries and the first white snow.
With night coming early and dawn coming late,
And ice in the bucket and frost by the gate.
The fires burn and kettles sing
And earth sinks to rest until next spring.
-Clyde Watson

THE FULL MOON IN NOVEMBER

The November full moon is called the *Beaver Moon*. Beavers were important to Native Americans and early pioneers who hunted them for food and used their skins to sell or trade. The traps were set before the ponds froze to ensure a supply of warm winter furs.

> *Black and icy pond*
> *Mirrors moon so round,*
> *While hidden in the beaver's lodge*
> *Coziness abounds.*
> "When the Moon is Full" by Penny Pollack

The November full moon is also called *The Frosty Moon*. Our first frost and first hard freeze have come and gone this month, and the leaves have blown off the trees.

IN THE GARDEN IN NOVEMBER

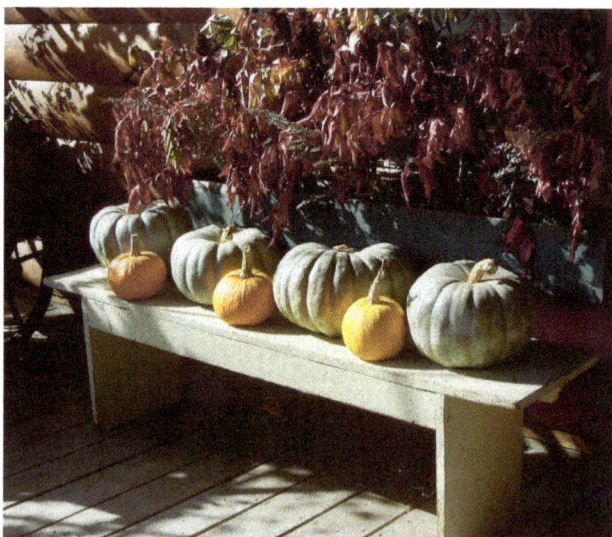

The first few pleasant days of November, I quickly put a few more bulbs into the earth, although it is a little late in the season. When spring comes I am always thankful to see the first blooms of daffodil, tulips, crocus and snowdrops, so I plant a few more bulbs late fall each year. It is a gift I give myself.

This late autumn, I brought in the pots of scented geranium and they now sit in a sunny south window. I enjoy their varied leaf shapes and delightful aromas. They are a tender perennial, so cannot be left outside in the winter. I love seeing something growing and green inside during the winter months. I do not grow these scented geraniums for their flowers, as the flowers are small and not showy, but enjoy the lemon or rose scent of their leaves when rubbed, uplifting my spirits on a gray and dreary day in November.

MULLING SPICES
2 T. cinnamon chips (*I use cinnamon sticks and roll firmly with rolling pin for chips*)
2 T. orange rind
4 tsp. whole allspice
4 tsp. whole cloves
1 tsp. to 1 T. brown sugar
1-2 drops vanilla

Put all in a muslin bag. Add to 2 quarts apple cider and simmer 30 minutes.

STOVETOP SIMMERING SPICES
3 c. water
2 T. whole cloves
1 T. whole allspice
2 cinnamon sticks
Dried orange, lemon or apple peel saved from peeling scraps

Put all ingredients in a pan on stove (*or mini crockpot*). Bring to boil and simmer for a delightful cozy scent in the air. (Do not drink this – it is an air scent only)

IN THE KITCHEN IN NOVEMBER

*T*hanksgiving Day is a day for eating as well as for gratitude. Our family has the traditional Thanksgiving meal with turkey and all the side dishes. I grew up with my mom making a German apple dressing made in a casserole instead of stuffed in the turkey. After I married, I wanted to continue that tradition, but could not make it quite like mom did, and my husband preferred the sage dressing his mom always made. So I learned to make my mom-in-law's sage dressing. Our kids loved it, and this is the only dressing they remember – a tradition continued from their father's side of the family.

Most families have their favorite traditional Thanksgiving recipes, and through the years the recipes are tweaked and changed, but the memories remain the same. Thanksgiving is a time I greatly look forward to, as I enjoy being in the kitchen and preparing the Thanksgiving meal for others. It is a simple pleasure and blessing in my life.

SAGE DRESSING
1 loaf stale bread, torn into small pieces
1 medium to large onion, finely diced

2 eggs, beaten
1 lb. sausage (not cooked), cut or torn in small chunks
1 ½ c. celery, finely diced
1 tsp. crumbled dried sage, rolled between hands to crumble
2 tsp. poultry seasoning
1 to 2 c. chicken broth

Put all together in a large bowl and mix with hands. Add enough broth to wet the dressing well but not soggy (the sausage creates moisture also). Put into large covered casserole for 30 t0 45 minutes. Then uncover and bake for another 30 t0 45 minutes.

CRANBERRY APPLE CRISP

Cranberries are abundant around Thanksgiving as they are a seasonal food (but almost impossible to find a month later) so in November, at Thanksgiving time, I stock up on cranberries, buying several extra bags and putting them in the freezer for later use.

6 large apples, sliced
1 c. fresh cranberries
TOPPING:
3/4 c. brown sugar, firmly packed
1/2 c. flour
1/2 c. oatmeal
3/4 tsp. cinnamon
1/2 tsp. nutmeg
1/3 c. softened butter

Preheat oven to 350 degrees. Butter a 9x9 inch square baking dish. Place apple slices and cranberries in baking dish. Mix remaining ingredients well and sprinkle over fruit. Bake 35-40 minutes. Best if served warm with ice cream. Serves 4-5. Double the recipe for a 9x13 pan.

GERMAN FRUITCAKE

I have been making this fruitcake every holiday season for many years. The recipe came from a neighbor who lived in Germany for several years and while there acquired the recipe. I did not grow up eating fruitcake during the holiday season, but it soon became a tradition when we started our own family.

This fruitcake does not have the usual citron in it, which many find bitter. It is important to buy the candied fruit the first of November, as it is usually sold out in most grocery stores after Thanksgiving. I make my own combination of candied fruit using candied pineapple and green candied cherries to avoid the citron and make this fruitcake around Thanksgiving, store in the refrigerator, and bring it out near Christmas.

2 sticks butter
1 ¼ c. sugar
5 eggs, room temperature
1/4 c. real maple syrup
1/2 c. milk or orange juice
2 ¼ c. all-purpose flour
1/4 tsp. salt
1 tsp. baking powder
1/4 tsp. cinnamon
1/8 tsp. allspice
1 ½ c. candied fruit mix (w/o citron or make own combination)
4 oz. red candied cherries, cut up
1 c. golden raisins
1 c. chopped dates (I buy pre-chopped)
2 c. pecans, coarsely chopped
1 c. English walnuts, coarsely chopped
1 tsp. vanilla

Preheat oven to 250 degrees. In a very big bowl beat together butter and sugar. Add eggs, one at a time, then syrup and liquid. Add dry ingredients and mix together. Add rest of ingredients. I start out using a mixer but switch to a big spoon to fold in nuts and fruits.

Makes 2 medium-size glass bread pans. Grease and flour, then cut a piece of parchment paper to line the pan. Grease and flour the paper also to make easy removal of fruitcake. This batter does not raise much when baked.

Bake for 2½ to 3 hours, depending on size of loaf pan used. Low heat and long baking time — do not over bake. Check with a toothpick that comes out clean for doneness at 2 ½ hours. Let cool completely, remove from pan and remove the paper liner. Store in refrigerator in plastic zipper bag. It will keep 8 weeks or freeze. Fruitcake develops its full flavor after being in refrigerator at least two weeks for the flavors to pull through.

BEING THANKFUL

I look for the blessings of the universe in each and every day. Some days I have to look longer, but I always know the blessings are there. I once read an article that recommended before going to bed each night to think about five good things one had experienced in the day, not including family or friends, as those are a given. This would be five things to be thankful for that day – I call them blessings – something similar to a gratitude journal, however this is not about writing it down, although that is still a good idea. This was about the *thought process* in one's mind each night after shutting the lights off and before falling asleep, counting blessings instead of the proverbial sheep!

I find when I do this daily, I become more aware and mindful of what goes on around me on a daily basis. I live more intentionally. When I become so busy that I go through life in a daze, it is good to slow down enough to mull around in my mind what I have experienced in the day and what I am thankful for. I believe that this is one of the very best things we can do in life – thinking about and writing down our blessings of the day.

SOME OF MY BLESSINGS DURING THE YEAR SO FAR:

• The pitter-patter of gentle raindrops falling against the window and knowing the earth is being watered by Mother Nature

• Checking on Mrs. Brown Thrush, sitting on her well-hidden nest in the wisteria-covered arbor this last summer

• The almost indescribable taste of the wild elderberry jelly on my toast this morning from the berries picked in summer and preserved

• Opening my front door to the fresh cool air that I inhaled deeply before 6 a.m. this morning

• Lighting a candle on a rainy day and taking time to reflect

THINKING ABOUT OR WRITING THE BLESSINGS I encounter during the day is now a nightly ritual. I turn the light off and mull the blessings of the day around in my mind, and I am thankful.

WILD TURKEYS

❧

*W*ild turkeys were never seen when I was growing up in the country. They were a rarity, and I had lived more than four decades before I saw a flock in a small clearing along a creek. What a joy! I was elated beyond words.

Later I began to see more wild turkeys here and there, and I would watch for them when traveling the countryside. I felt they were so much a part of what makes up *country* that they should have been there all along. I did not realize that in the past they had been hunted so profusely they almost disappeared from the land.

Most children today know the meat on the table on Thanksgiving Day is turkey, and in school they trace the outline of their hand to form a turkey as an art project. But they know very little about the bird or where it comes from. Since I didn't grow up with turkeys around me, I felt I needed to learn more about them.

Wild turkeys are native to North America. They became scarce as they were hunted for food for the table until the tame turkeys were grown in large farm operations, replacing wild turkey as the meat for Thanksgiving dinners. The population of wild turkeys has now recovered in all states except Alaska.

Wild turkeys look like slow moving big birds, but in reality they can fly quite well. They have a wingspan of 4 feet and can live to 10 years, and at night will fly into the trees to roost. Their diet consists of nuts, berries, snails, insects and grains in the fields.

The males have a bristly *beard* that grows from the chest, and begin their courtship with the females in March and April. The male turkeys will puff up the feathers on their bodies and *gobble* loudly and often. I was amazed to learn turkeys have 5,000 to 6,000 dark feathers. Hen turkeys will make their nest in tall grasses and have a clutch of one to two dozen eggs, laying one a day, and the chicks will hatch in 28 days. When the turkeys are young and cannot fly they are most vulnerable to predators, including coyotes, bobcats, owls and of course, humans.

Turkeys can be territorial and aggressive. My neighbor, Sue, came home from work one day and a group of wild turkeys from the creek nearby would not let her in her home. They aggressively protected the front porch. Her husband arrived home and scared the turkeys away from the house.

In my woods, I have seen one lone female turkey fairly often. She has been around for the last several years and meanders the woods and around the lake and creek nearby. I have spotted her in the woods when walking down my country lane and I talk to her. I ask her, *"Why are you all alone?"* and I tell her, *"I understand."* I tell her to *"Be safe,"* and I will put cranberries and nuts out for her to eat. She nods her head and continues her walk, and I do too.

My hope is that upcoming generations will have more of a connection to the earth and her wild creatures, so the wisdom of the wild is not lost forever.

December

THE VIEW FROM MY WINDOW

On the first day of winter,
the earth awakens to the cold touch of itself.
Snow knows no other recourse except this falling,
this sudden letting go over the small bushes,
all the emptying trees.
Snow puts beauty back into the withered and malnourished,
into the death-wish of nature
and the way winter insists on nothing deliberate
less than difference, waiting all its life;
snow says, "Let me cover you."
–Laura Lush, The First Day of Winter

*O*h, the peacefulness of winter!

The morning snow is drifting down to the earth slowly, like fluffy feathers being shaken out of an old goose feather pillow, and settles on the twigs and branches like icing on a cake. It changes the hushed landscape, and I silently watch as the woods become ghostly white. The pristine whiteness is beautiful, and I am in awe of this moment in time. And later, after the snow stops, I'll venture out into a clean and lovely blanket of white covering

317

the earth. I am looking forward to breathing in the fresh crisp and clean air. My breath stops for a minute as a flash of red lands on the arbor – a fire red cardinal. How wonderful to see these beautiful birds in this winter wonderland, so striking against the newly fallen white snow. It is a picture-taking moment in my mind, and a simple blessing I savor. Mother Nature always inspires me.

Winter waves a magic wand over this world, and behold, everything is softer and more beautiful!
– Norman Vincent Peale

Many December days are dreary, dark and gloomy, when the weather cannot decide if it should rain or snow or settle for something in between. It is cloudy and cold today. Gazing out my big south window looking out to the wooded hills beyond, I expect snow flurries any minute as the weatherman has predicted, but we know Mother Nature has a mind of her own and works on her own timetable.

The early hours of the morning beckon when the world is quiet all around me. Once again I hear the familiar hoot owl at 6 a.m. hooting out his *good morning* call. I like to think he is checking on me at this early hour. I would love to *hoot* back and connect with this friendly owl that seems to have claimed my little corner of the world for his home too. Once in a while, in the early morning dawn, I slip out the back door and see him sitting on top of my fireplace chimney surveying the woods all around. He must be used to me gazing at him in wonder, as he does not spook easily, and I am grateful. I suspect he is looking for his breakfast in the coldness of this early morning, and I quietly go back inside to fix my own breakfast. The owls ground and connect me to the earth, and hearing him hoot close by, I quietly ask him to visit often.

The freshly fallen snow is nudging me gently into a holiday spirit. The tall slender Christmas tree looks like a Colorado green spruce in the corner of the family room, covered with tiny lights and no decorations. Before the tree was in its corner spot, I gathered together the new tiny clear bright lights I had purchased and gave them a quick coating of spray frost. I prefer not having gaudy bright lights glaring at me as if I am at a carnival. The frost spray makes them look just right – a little subdued. I add no ornaments to the tree except a bird nest tucked into the branches and a little cloth bird. My preference is a simple look and as natural as possible. I add fresh cedar to the mantle of the fireplace as I do every year, and the scent is lovely. Fresh cedar is placed around a jar candle and twig wreath in the center of the table, and sprigs are tucked in here and there on the bookcase shelves. A few of the smaller cedar branches will be used to make cedar bundles for the fireplace and for gift giving. I light the cinnamon and cloves candle, turn a little holiday music low so it won't interrupt my thoughts, and then finish addressing the annual letter and cards to send to family and friends near and far. Most of the gifts are handmade from cloth and paper, and I add a food item or two. All seem to be appreciated by the receivers with joy from the giver. Handmade gifts are truly gifts from the heart. Family and friends agree now that we no longer need the gifts – only the gift of time with each other.

The only true gift is a portion of thyself.
–Emerson

The best gifts are tied with heartstrings.
– Unknown

Blessed is the season which engages the whole world in a conspiracy of love.
–Hamilton Wright Mabil

319

Somehow not only this season
But all the year through
The Joy that you give to others
Is the joy that comes back to you.
– John Greenleaf Whittier

Solstice means *"sun-stop,"* and Winter Solstice is the longest night of the year. The animals rest more and the plants have already sent their energy underground to the roots. It is a time of dreaming about seeds I will plant in the garden in the coming spring and projects to do. Solstice has been celebrated throughout time as a return of the light and the rebirth of the sun. It is the time when the days begin to get longer, lighter and brighter, and I welcome it.

It is important to keep our rituals and traditions, and I continue this ancient tradition of celebrating the holiday of the changing season. I sometimes think we are in a bit of conflict and contradiction during the month of December. It is the hibernation time when our bodies need more rest and regeneration, but our holiday rituals have us running around exhausted and busier than any other time of year. Sometimes sickness settles in from lack of rest, eating too many sweets and in general too much *hustle and bustle* during the season of Yule. As the years pass, I choose the rituals most important to me and give up the others. I work at finding balance continually, and especially with my December rituals. I keep my herbal remedies close at hand to help my immune system stay strong so I can enjoy the beauty and blessings of December.

Sometimes traditions are worth reviving – The old European
custom of using rosemary at Christmas is one.
– Tom DeBaggio

We near the end of a busy month in December and another year is coming to an end. I remind myself how important it is in the winter to find more balance and peace. Sometimes I sit still, watching the flames in the fireplace dance up the chimney and let go of my many thoughts running around in my busy brain. Gazing out my big south window with its ever-changing view of the hills beyond gives me balance time and again, and I slow down, mentally and physically.

The winter sunset colors of gold, red and peach are spectacular, and every night is different. I take a moment each evening to enjoy the sunset while sitting in the old rocker on the big front porch on the west side of my home. The December sunsets seem to be the most dramatic of the year, and I have often thought of making a picture journal of the thirty-one evening sunsets in December. It would be a joy to do, but pictures cannot fully capture Mother Nature's beauty. The sunsets are a reminder for me to take the time for a mindful moment and truly see Mother Nature's beauty all around. Nature is a healer. I am part of it, and soon the season will be gone.

The mountain, I am part of it....
The herbs, the fir tree —
I am part of it.
The morning mists, the clouds, the gathering waters —
I am part of it.
The wilderness, the dew drops, the pollen —
I am part of it.
- Navajo, traditional chant

I look out to the backyard in the morning and am saddened to notice there are not as many birds around my feeders as in the years before. I feed and water, but there seem to be fewer and fewer birds. I wonder as I do so often these days: is it drought, global warming, or the pesticides and herbicides used so freely that are destroying them, as well as summer's butterflies and bees? It is probably all these things put together, and I miss them. It is cause for concern. The creatures I once enjoyed seeing in the meadow and garden in great abundance are now few and far between. I cannot imagine not seeing and enjoying birds in winter, or all year around here in my home in the woods.

I heard a bird sing
In the dark of December
A magical thing
And sweet to remember.
We are nearer to Spring
Than we were in September,
I heard a bird sing
In the dark of December.
– Oliver Herford, *I Heard a Bird Sing*

It is the end of December and the morning chores are done. I decide to have my second cup of hot herbal tea – Earl Grey and lavender for me today. I pull up an old Windsor-style chair and sit awhile by the big south window in quiet meditation and reflection. It is the time of year when I reflect how the ending year has been and what has been accomplished. And tentatively, I make a few resolutions for the new year fast approaching.

New Year's Eve arrives as it does every December 31st. I have heard said that the days go slow but the years go fast, and this one has passed by ever so quickly. Where did it go and what did I do? Did I challenge myself to grow and learn? Did I accomplish what I wanted to do? Did I take time for myself? Did I learn more about awareness, mindfulness and gratitude?

In the new year ahead, I wish everyone a kinder and gentler way of life, a slower pace of daily living with Nature as our partner, and a front porch to view it all from. My hope is that we can all live more meaningful and mindful lives. I wish for less violence and more kindness in the world, and peace, hope, love, gratitude and harmony for all. I wish for a New Year full of contentment and joy, full of magic and wonder, and for simple pleasures that can be found right outside our door every month of the year.

Let there be peace on earth and let it begin with me,
Let there be peace on earth, the peace that was meant to be.
– Sy Miller and Jill Jackson

THE FULL MOON IN DECEMBER

amidst the hustle and bustle of December, I stop for a moment in time to stand outside and talk to the full *Cold Moon* of December. It is very cold this evening, and I am bundled up for my visit with the moon.

During the month of December, the winter cold tightens its grip and nights are at their coldest and longest. The December full moon is also called the *Long Night Full Moon*, appropriately named for the midwinter night that is indeed long, and the moon hangs in the sky for a longer time. It was also called the *Moon before Yule*.

IN THE GARDEN IN DECEMBER

Sleep well, my garden, while the snow blankets your roots.

I talk to my winter plants as I meander through the garden path in December. The plants are in hibernation too. I clip a few dried stems and add them to a bowl of potpourri.

> *Come into the Christmas garden*
> *That groweth all the year,*
> *And makes perfume*
> *For all your rooms*
> *And herbs for Yuletide Cheer!*
> -Adelma Grenier Simmons, a fine old herbwoman

HOLIDAY GARDEN POTPOURRI

(I choose what I want to add and dry these during the late summer months to use in winter)

1/2 c. juniper/cedar berries

1/2 c. juniper/cedar fresh greenery

1 c. rosemary, dried (strip from branches while fresh, then dry)

1 c. very small pinecones

1 c. dried orange peel pieces

1 to 2 c. dried rose petals

1/2 c. cinnamon chips (or sticks broken into pieces)

2 tsp. orris root pieces (a scent fixative – put the essential oils on the orris root)

Essential oil is optional:

12 drops orange essential oil

6 drops cinnamon essential oil

4 drops rosemary essential oil

4 drops clove essential oil

Put all into a glass jar with lid or a covered glass container. Allow a couple of weeks for the scent to draw through. Place in an open glass bowl for display. Because of the added essential oils, I do not put into a wooden bowl, but instead I use an old white ironstone bowl. A white ironstone platter would be pretty too, with a candle in the middle, protected by a glass chimney and adding a few whole sprigs of rosemary.

SPICED HONEY

I love spiced honey. To make it, I use raw organic honey, cinnamon sticks, a few cloves, and a crushed cardamom pod.

Gently warm the honey and pour over these strong spices. Let set 2 weeks before using so flavors can draw through. This is a special winter delight when put on toast, into a cup of tea, or drizzled over a baked apple.

IN THE KITCHEN IN DECEMBER

REFRIGERATED BUTTER PECAN COOKIES

This is a holiday favorite and a good cookie dough to make ahead and freeze. Slice off and bake when needed. The recipe was my Aunt Verda's favorite and was given to me by my mom, keeper of family recipes.

1 c. butter, browned
2 c. brown sugar
2 eggs, beaten
1 tsp. maple flavoring
1 c. pecans, finely chopped
3 c. flour
1 tsp. soda
1 tsp. cream of tartar
Dash salt

Preheat oven to 350 degrees. Melt butter and brown in small skillet, watching it closely so it doesn't burn. Pour over the brown sugar. Mix in rest of ingredients. Make dough into a 2-inch roll, wrapping in wax paper or plastic and chill several hours or overnight. Slice off cookies and bake 10 minutes. When the edges start to brown remove cookies from oven. I have frozen the dough logs for 2-3 months and love the convenience of having them handy to slice and bake.

MAPLE/CINNAMON PECANS
4 T. (half stick) butter
1/4 c. brown sugar, packed
1/4 c. Real maple syrup
3 c. pecan halves
1/8 tsp. cinnamon

Preheat oven to 250 degrees. Melt all ingredients except pecans over medium heat together in pan. When melted, add pecans and cook 2- 3 minutes stirring constantly. Pour onto parchment-lined cookie sheet and sprinkle lightly with sea salt. Bake for 15 minutes. Remove from oven, stir through pecans, sprinkle with salt lightly again and cool. Great for party, snacking and general gift giving.

'TIS THE SEASON

SLEDS

I love sleds. Perhaps it is the childhood memories of going fast down a hill. Sleds evoke wonderful thoughts of sledding when I was small and also with my children as they were growing up. I am not fond of plastic new sleds, preferring the old sleds with their steel runners and wood tops.

In December, I like to prop an old sled by my front door, hang a wreath or cedar sprigs on it, along with a pair of woolen mittens. The sled brings a smile to the face of visitors coming to my home. I wish I still had my old childhood sled, but there probably wasn't much of it left, as I was the oldest of six children in my family. Instead, I went to a farm auction where I found an old sled with original red paint still on it. I also found a very small child's sled to use on a table or my kitchen island as a seasonal centerpiece with a glowing candle inside a wreath on top. I have also used the small sled as a serving piece for a plate of frosted sugar cookies. Decorating my home this way brings comments of appreciation from my friends and joy to my heart to have these items repurposed, used and on display.

WOODEN BOWLS

Wooden bowls are made to hold something — whatever we want them to hold. They come in all sizes, plain or with old paint on them. During the holiday season I add fresh-cut greenery from the juniper/cedar trees and tuck in fresh fruit like oranges, apples or pomegranates. Sometimes I stick in a couple of candy canes for a more festive look, or change it out with fresh limes and cinnamon sticks. An old wooden bowl will also hold candies and cookies, which my grandkids love.

FIREPLACE MANTEL

The mantel of my fireplace is a wonderful spot to add greenery for the season. How festive it looks once the fragrant greenery is put in place! When my fireplace surround was built, I requested an electric outlet on the mantel. I can plug in festive lights and the outlet is never seen, as it is painted the color of the walls. When I don't have a string of lights up for holiday décor, I always have a small electric candlestick on each side. Greenery and lights are the first step decorating the mantel, and then I add a nutcracker or two or chalkware Santas. I put a small branch of fresh greenery into each of two terracotta flower pots, placing them on each side of the mantel for height, making them look like topiaries. After the holiday, I exchange the Santas and nutcrackers for snowmen, still festive and winter-themed. It is satisfying to have items from Mother Nature in my home during the winter season as part of my décor.

LUMINARIAS

I have a winding walkway leading to my front door, and I like to make luminarias when guests are expected in the evenings. These are made using canning jars or repurposed food jars. I have used them plain, but usually I spray the jars with glass frost, available from a craft store. Inside the jar, I place 2-3 inches of sand or Epsom salt and set a small votive candle or a 6-hour tea light candle into the sand/salt. I line a side of the walkway with the luminarias and light them fifteen minutes before guests arrive for a welcoming invitation to my home.

POTPOURRI

I enjoy a bowl of potpourri sitting around at holiday time. Most of the potpourri one can buy now has an overpowering synthetic fragrance, so I make my own. I place a jar candle in the middle of a wooden bowl and add dried berries, rose hips, little pine cones, and seed pods all around it. I save the peels of an apple and orange, tearing them into pieces the size of a quarter, letting them dry well before adding to the potpourri for color and natural scent. A few drops of clove or cinnamon essential oil will enhance the fragrance, but I don't use essential oil in a wooden bowl, as it will absorb the oil and scent, so I use a pottery bowl instead. I purchase a few miniature limes from the produce aisle to add to the bowl for color and interest. This is a natural potpourri that can be added to during the winter months and enjoyed all season long.

CEDAR BUNDLES

I make up small cedar bundles to burn in my fireplace as fire starter in the winter. These can also be used as a smudge stick if the cedar and other herbs are wrapped very tightly. The cedar is considered an ancient and wise tree. Traditionally, cedar was used to cleanse the air and for purification to drive away negative energy. Dried cedar is highly flammable, so one must be careful in wrapping it right while still green or use a small amount of cedar along with dried rosemary and sage.

I LIKE TO KEEP MY HOLIDAY DECORATING SIMPLE AND natural. The season has become commercialized and full of plastics and *stuff* in general, doing nothing to enhance our celebration of the natural season. I edit out what is not important to me, and find items from nature feed my spirit the most during wintertime and all year 'round.

PINE SCENTED POTPOURRI

1/2 c. bay leaves
1/2 c. balsam needles
1/2 c. mini pine cones
1/2 c. dried rose hips
1 T. orris root (for holding the scent)
10-20 drops fir or pine essential oil

WINTER SPICES

Simmering spices are nice to give as a small hostess gift. Here's how I do it: I put the dried items together in a cellophane bag along with a fresh orange and tie with a red ribbon. The tag instructions say: *"Quarter the orange, place all in small saucepan or little crock pot. Add the spices. Fill the pan with water and bring to a boil, then simmer on lowest setting, watching so the water does not go dry. Add water as needed. Use in a day or two or refrigerate up to a week (fresh fruit will mold)."*

The spices are:
1 T. each of whole allspice, whole cloves, cinnamon pieces

1 T. orange rind (I make small stars from the rind with a 1- inch cookie cutter and let dry)
A handful pine needles
Optional: fresh or dried apple slices, fresh cranberries, fresh grated nutmeg

Notes:

When eating a lot of citrus during the winter, I like to save the peels to use fresh or dried in a simmering pot on the stove or a mini crock pot. Add spices to water and the citrus peel for a delightful fragrance that will fill the air and uplift winter spirits. I always choose organic citrus and wash the peel before peeling the fruit. I use fresh or dry the peel, and love having it available for flavoring in teas and jellies.

Using purchased fresh holiday greenery is not recommended for decorating or potpourri, as they have been sprayed with chemical fragrance/preservative. Use within one or two days or refrigerate up to a week. Otherwise fresh fruits will mold.

NATIVE RED CEDAR TREE

The native Red Cedar tree (*Juniperus virginiana*) is the bane of many farmers with pastures. The little seedlings pop up everywhere, and farmers systematically chop them out every few years. If they did not do this, the cedars would create a snug and cozy forest in no time at all. It is a survivor tree and can take extremes in temperature – sometimes quite extreme. Our weather can be harsh with hot dry winds and temperatures climbing to 101 in the shade, and in the winter the wind chills can be minus 20 degrees or colder. But Cedar survives, providing shelter for all.

When my husband and I were first married and could not afford to buy a Christmas tree, we would go into the pasture or along the roadside to cut down a tree and bring it into the house a few days before the holiday. The little prairie Red Cedar was our Christmas tree year after year, for many years. The tree was so prickly that we could barely put a string of lights on it, but it made a charming holiday tree for our little home. To this day, I believe it was my favorite holiday tree of all, perhaps because life was simpler then. And it is the simple things of life that are the best and most memorable.

In Nebraska, our old cedars grew along a fence row where birds had dropped the seed a long time ago. But in two other fence rows we planted little seedlings we dug from a pasture. We planted the baby trees in hopes that one day they would create a nice windbreak, a delineation of property lines, as well as provide a sanctuary for birds and animals.

We watered the baby trees well the first year, and they soon were three-feet tall. Planting the trees was a good decision, although over the years I pulled many little four-inch Cedar seedlings out of the herb garden, vegetable garden and even the lawn. If a seedling was a foot-tall, I knew the root was that long too, and would dig them out of an unwanted place, putting them in a can or plastic jug to give away to someone who wanted a Cedar tree. Surprisingly, I always had takers.

I have always called Cedar a sacred tree. Her dense branches shelter wildlife. I can envision a mama deer giving birth to her baby under its big branches. Cedar adapts to where she is. The little blue berries (actually cones) readily self-seed. When planted along a perimeter or fence row, Cedar will make a dense fortress and produce little trees all around it from its seeds, creating a community. Cedar has also been called the *Tree of Protection*.

When settlers came to this land they had a hard time surviving the ice and snow and long winters, but Native Americans taught them about wild plants and trees. Without Vitamin C, they would not survive the winter, so they learned about boiling down cedar bark to get this lifesaving nutrition into their bodies. The Cedar lives a long time and is a symbol of longevity. I lovingly call her the *Tree of Life*.

Being a survivalist tree, Cedar has very deep roots and no leaf surface to speak of. The needles (leaves) can sometimes be prickly, making me take notice. She is telling me to *stand back – respect me*, and I do. I ask her permission before gathering the greens for my

December decorating. The greens have started turning a russet brown from the drying winter winds. Cedar is a tree that grows quickly and can reach 75 feet tall in some places with a width up to 50 feet. She has a pungent odor, but I do not find it offensive.

I have always been drawn to Red Cedar, and when I was a student in a class given by noted author and herbalist Stephen Buhner, we were to choose a plant/tree we wanted to spend an hour with, sitting beside her and listening to her. A Red Cedar native tree drew me like a magnet, and I sat with her and wrote my impressions as we connected as two related beings.

When I moved to my current home in the woods, I was happy to see Red Cedars lining one side of the long lane, plus a mini-forest of Cedar trees on the edge of the woods. I knew there would be many birds in this area, as well as wildlife, because of the Cedar trees. I felt the red cedars were lined up along the long lane like friends waiting to welcome me home.

IN CLOSING

To laugh often and much,
To win the respect of intelligent people and the affection of children,
To leave the world a better place,
To know even one life has breathed easier because you have lived.
This is to have succeeded.
-Ralph Waldo Emerson

I have been curious all my life, asking *how and why* since I was a small child. I questioned many things, like *why is it this way and not another way?* I would either voice the questions out loud or sometimes I would silently ask my inner self the question and then seek the answer.

In nature, I found there were fewer questions. I accepted the trees growing in the woods, noting the regional differences in the many places I lived. I accepted the rocks, the soil of the earth, the wild flowers growing. I understood the need for the spider to spin a big web to retrieve its next meal. I understood the camouflage color of the fur coat of the deer to hide itself in the woods from the hunter. But the mysteries still prevailed, and also the contradictions.

I loved growing up in the country. When I married and had children, I heard a lot of talk about a book called *Silent Spring*, authored by Rachel Carson. I read it and it changed my life. There were questions in the book, and also predictable answers, and I began to care deeply for Mother Earth, not taking her for granted as I did as a child. After reading the book, I knew that what we did to Mother Earth we did to ourselves. I learned that the planet we call *HOME* might be destroyed one day by mankind, but more than likely Mother Earth will survive and we will destroy ourselves.

I listen to the drumming – the heartbeat of Mother Earth. What is she telling us? I want to mindfully listen and enjoy Mother Earth daily as long as she is here and I am here. I forage for my medicine and plant food. I am thankful for the wildness of the Earth. I know we must be good stewards, because our lives truly depend on it.

When my daughter was in high school, many years ago, a teacher made a statement that made a big impression on her. The instructor told his students *one day there will be water wars – wars over water usage.* And today we are fighting and protesting to protect our water rights – to prevent the oil giants from putting big pipelines under major rivers for fear of leaking into the water millions of people drink. The peaceful protest at Standing Rock (in North Dakota) in 2016 brought to light the fear and concern of many people who want to protect our water rights and respect sacred land. I fear we, the common people who love the earth, will lose in the end. Big government and big corporations with big money will eventually destroy what we hold sacred – life itself. We will put up a good fight.

Wars are now fought over oil. Global warming is happening. There will be consequences. Some things can be fixed but most I fear will not. We cannot go back and we all will lose.

Sometimes life is bleak and depressing when we look at the big picture and what is happening with Mother Earth – our home. We have to have hope. We send prayers out into the Universe for common sense and protection of our natural resources. And in the meantime, without hiding our heads in the sand and continually being aware, we take pride and find peace in our own little corners of the world — be it a piece of land or a park to walk in. For those fortunate enough to have a piece of Mother Earth to reside upon, we must work to keep it pristine and untouched for the insects, plants, birds and roaming creatures to enjoy and survive — including us. Wherever we are is sacred ground – it is where we find solitude, acceptance and peace. It is where we learn about the cycles of life. I will forever be asking *how and why,* and will never understand it all.

Through this book, my hope to help everyone look at the world differently – to find peaceful places in nature and bring balance back into life, and to help future generations find harmony walking on Mother Earth. When we are present in the moment, it is amazing what we find when we listen and look around us. Giving ourselves space and time to do this creates awareness in every aspect of our life, and may be the most important thing we will ever do.

This little book has now found its end. It was a labor of love with labor pains lasting ten years before finally birthing into a book. These words come straight from my heart.

I give thanks to EVERYONE
who has been a part of my life's journey.
Good Earth Blessings, Twila

We are all part of the life cycle.
Like a seed we are born, we sprout, we grow, we mature
and later we decay and die,
making room for future generations who, like seedlings,
are reborn through us.
This is all part of nature's dance.
-Margo Adler

ONE DAY WHEN I AM GONE, I WANT THESE WORDS TO echo through the trees:

May the wind carry her spirit gently,
May the fire release her soul,
May the Universe rock her in loving arms
And may the wheel turn and bring her to rebirth.
-Starhawk

RESOURCES

A few of the many wonderful resources in my personal library I have used and continue to use:

Books on Herbs by:
Rosemary Gladstar
Stephen Harrod Buhner
Robin Rose Bennett
Matthew Wood
Michael Tierra
Susun Weed

Foraging and Feasting by Dina Falconi
Dandelion Medicine by Brigette Mars
A Kids Herb Book – for all ages by Lesley Tierra
Your Backyard Herb Garden by Miranda Smith

Other Books:
Silent Spring by Rachel Carson
Braiding Sweetgrass by Robin Wall Kimmerer
Dating Antique Quilts by Barbara Brackman
When the Moon is Full by Penny Pollack
Full Moon Lore by Ellen Wahi
Circle of Stones by Judith Duerk
Wool applique books by Maggie Bonanomi
My Nature Journal by Adrienne Olmstead
Wildflower Tea by Ethel Pochocki and Roger Essley
Bird Nests – a Peterson field guide
Landscaping in all Seasons by Masters
Winter Gardens by Cedric Pollet
The Winter Garden by Val Bourne
The Garden in Winter by Rosemary Verrey

DVD – *My Life as a Turkey* (documentary) by Joe Hutto

ABOUT THE AUTHOR

Twila K. Fairbanks is a seasoned shop owner, having had successful antique/gifts shops in Lincoln and Roca, Nebraska, and Estes Park, Colorado. She has taught primitive wool rug hooking, dyeing wool, wool appliqué, creating a healing garden, home herbalism, and an *Earth Connection* series of classes. Some of these are still ongoing, although Twila is mostly retired, living a simple and private life of peace and solitude in her home in the woods.

Twila is a granny woman and Earth Mother. Her passions today are many, including making herbal medicines, gardening, wool working with needle & thread, making pine needle baskets and being a keeper of the Earth.

Twila founded the *Log Cabin Herb Study Group* and the *Woolkeepers* rug hooking group in Nebraska. In Kansas, she co-founded the *Kaw Valley Herb Study Group* and the *Good Earth Gatherings* shop near Lawrence with her daughter, Tamara, and co-teaches a 10-month *Home Herbalism* course and other classes.

www.GoodEarthGatherings.com

(Signed copies of this book are available through the website above or contact Twila directly).

Twila's email: ladybuglady2013@gmail.com

www.ingramcontent.com/pod-product-compliance
Lightning Source LLC
Chambersburg PA
CBHW062107040426
42336CB00042B/2306